LEAD BIGGER

The Transformative Power of Inclusion

ANNE CHOW

SIMON & SCHUSTER

New York   London   Toronto   Sydney   New Delhi

1230 Avenue of the Americas
New York, NY 10020

First Simon & Schuster hardcover edition September 2024

SIMON & SCHUSTER and colophon are registered trademarks of Simon & Schuster, LLC

Simon & Schuster: Celebrating 100 Years of Publishing in 2024

For information about special discounts for bulk purchases, please contact Simon & Schuster Special Sales at 1-866-506-1949 or business@simonandschuster.com.

The Simon & Schuster Speakers Bureau can bring authors to your live event. For more information or to book an event, contact the Simon & Schuster Speakers Bureau at 1-866-248-3049 or visit our website at www.simonspeakers.com.

Interior design by Wendy Blum

Manufactured in the United States of America

1 3 5 7 9 10 8 6 4 2

Library of Congress Cataloging-in-Publication Data has been applied for.

ISBN 978-1-6680-2400-3
ISBN 978-1-6680-2402-7 (ebook)

To my parents, Dr. Ming-Chwan and Joann Chao-Chu Chow,
who showed me that bigger is always possible

CONTENTS

Part Four: Bigger Conversations

CHAPTER ONE

THE OPPORTUNITY TO LEAD BIGGER

One of the mementos from my career I'm proudest of is an old yellow mug with an expletive on it, gifted to me by a team who taught me a new way to lead. I rediscovered it as I was cleaning out my office after a thirty-plus-year corporate career at AT&T. The mug reminded me of an early but important experience that convinced me not to head down the well-worn, often micromanaged or uninspired path of other leaders. I wanted instead to curate an approach with a wider, more human perspective, something I've since come to call *leading bigger*.

Back in the day, if you wanted to climb the ladder at AT&T, you needed to prove yourself by leading a large team. My post was to manage a customer service organization of several hundred people across the United States who were responsible for the clients purchasing our 1-800 toll-free-number services.

Until that point, I'd managed only a couple of staff members located in the same office. To say I was nervous would be an understatement. What did a twenty-something know about supporting customers seven days a week, twenty-four hours a day, as the head of a demanding, diverse team whose members were twice my age and far more experienced?

I thankfully understood that, to start, I needed to listen to the people I was now responsible for. I met with many service representatives and technicians across locations, who didn't hesitate to provide their unvarnished feedback: *You're just a young whippersnapper.* (They really called me that, even though this was the 1990s, not the 1890s.) And *You're only here to get your large-team experience. Then you'll leave.* And *District managers like you come and go. We do the work, and managers haven't helped us improve anything at all.*

I expected straight talk, but I got more than I anticipated. Not that I could blame them. They expected a self-centered style of leader who came in and focused solely on the task at hand—prioritizing short-term results, treating them as expendable, and enforcing a rigid approach to the workplace that dampened human ingenuity.

In that moment, I could have wielded my formal authority. I was, after all, their boss. I could've pushed my team to hit our targets just long enough to be able to achieve my next career goal and move on. Others before me had done exactly that, leaving a skeptical workforce in their wake. But in my gut, I knew this wasn't how I wanted to lead. Even if relying on this authority structure was standard corporate behavior, it wasn't what my team needed or deserved.

After all, I was a daughter of immigrants raised to get along, fit in, and work hard to be respected, so this managerial approach, though common, was anathema to me. And as a second-generation Asian American—and often the first or only in any given environment—I struggled to belong. So I was acutely aware of the real challenges in fostering connection and community in my professional roles. Rather than pulling rank, I was inclined to do the opposite, because using hierarchy to drive behavior always felt small to me.

Instead, in what became a career-defining moment, I decided my top priority was to lead *bigger.* I wanted to win the respect of the team; I wanted us to collaborate. And I hoped that we could make enduring improvements together in ways that would be helpful to the larger company. I didn't want to selfishly check a box and move to my next assignment.

I did not have any sophisticated management model, but I did sense that to get to these bigger outcomes, I had to broaden my view to focus on the work, the people (the workforce), and the environment we were working in (the workplace). I knew gaining insights from others both inside and outside of my organization would be helpful, both to me as the leader and to my team. In my view, leading bigger was all about widening my perspectives by engaging with more people and taking in more information to elevate our performance and impact, helping my team deliver on a greater potential.

It also meant being a bigger person—caring about people and bringing a generous nature to work.

This is in contrast to small leadership, which I view as taking a narrow, one-dimensional, often short-term focus on a singular stakeholder or set of measures—usually financial. This approach is typically self-serving and less collaborative.

Little did I know that my predisposition to lead bigger was really about inclusive leadership, but at the time I was still formulating this principle. I knew I wanted to spark connection and inspiration in the work, and with the people in and around it. This included not just the employees but also our customers and the communities in which we operated—the groups that today I'd call stakeholders. I believed there was a way to compel all these people to meaningfully contribute, and for some, to band together in our human desire to belong. I wanted my team to know that I saw and respected them as human beings, so they in turn could bring their whole selves to work, perform their best, and realize their fullest potential. I wanted a workplace culture that cultivated innovation through strong trust and camaraderie, not one organized to bolster my own sense of ego or control.

I initially took the job thinking I was going to manage the customer service team, but I suddenly found myself in charge of addressing all the problems coming our way not only from the customers themselves but also from the rest of the organization. I first came to this realization in the confines of a stuffy windowless conference room, gathered around my new leadership team for the first time. They had clearly prepared for this gathering, and the most tenured manager of the bunch, a salty gentle-man more than thirty years my senior, with his entire career spent in the same work center, had been nominated as spokesperson. He proceeded to lecture me, itemizing several points: "Our people are so dedicated, it's amazing they can get the job done without any support from headquarters. We're in this alone; no one else is working 24-7 on the phones taking customer calls. So many groups take advantage of us, and there aren't any consequences for how crappy they treat us." It didn't take long for the ten other people in the room to energetically pile on with their own examples and emotions. I might've been the boss, but I was clearly also the student.

So I went to school. One of the biggest barriers to delivering a consistent satisfactory customer experience was the sales teams. Every day my team took calls from salespeople who made urgent requests ranging from "My customer needs this service to be turned on this week. I know I haven't given you the order yet, but I need you to get it done. Otherwise we'll lose the business" to "Why isn't my customer's service back up yet? What's taking you so long?" to "What do you mean that can't get done? I already told the customer we can do it." In all cases, large fissures between the sales and service teams rose to the surface. It was as if they thought we didn't care about the customer, and they didn't behave like we were part of the same company. These haphazard behaviors caused major pain for my team and hurt their ability to do their work well.

I had to champion their needs on behalf of the business. I wasn't just responsible for getting the job done, I was responsible for the people doing the job. It didn't take long to gather the data from my team; they knew which sales organizations were chronic offenders. I understood that I had to go beyond my own group to improve the impact we were having on our customers and on the growth of our business. Imagine me, mid-twenties, standing at five-foot-three (ish), challenging the most difficult sales leader because I figured that if I could get him on the same page, the other conversations would go more smoothly. This guy stood a foot taller than me and had of course many more years in the company, and I dreaded confronting him. But I strolled into his office with conviction. As I brought the issues up, he denied any culpability: "Anne, that's just the way it works around here. We can't control what our customers want." We went back and forth several times. "Anne, come on. Do you really think my team is trying to make things worse?" As I calmly gave him example after example of poor partnership, lack of communication, and the harm it was wreaking on our customers, he sheepishly admitted, "Okay, maybe you have a point. Customers could benefit from a better handoff. Let's try it." In retrospect, I was trying to get him to *lead bigger* with me. Ultimately we delivered better results as we began to share accountability for the customer experience and gained more trust in each other. Together, we created an environment where sales and service worked hand in hand. As this sales leader and I improved our collaboration, our teams followed suit. Interestingly, this sales/customer service model is now used across many industries to ensure customer-centric growth.

I championed my group's needs, removing other structural barriers while also advocating for them and working with them to unlock their—and my—potential. This meant that I had to lead bigger beyond my job description—managing the customer service team—and focus strategically on the work, the workforce, and the workplace. It was clear to me that while our duties (work) were why we were there, we wouldn't be able to do our best if I, as the leader, didn't prioritize my people's issues and needs (workforce) while ensuring that their environment was designed to enable them to succeed (workplace).

Shortly after I started, several technicians bet me that I wouldn't last six months. I wound up serving in that leadership role for three years. During this time, we came together as a team, learning from our mistakes and celebrating our successes. We bonded not just as professionals but as people, who faced mental health challenges, security threats, and family milestones together.

This brings me back to my treasured coffee cup. When I eventually moved from that assignment, I had a series of closure sessions with my employees, thanking them for their dedication, contributions, and willingness to teach me while reinforcing the importance of their roles to our customers and in the growth of our business. To my surprise, one of the technicians presented me with a yellow mug that read: "Boys I'm Taking

Charge Here" (spelled out vertically, with emphasis on the first letter of each word). I was truly touched and found it hilarious. At the time, the legal team was particularly sensitive about the acronym and asked me not to broadcast this story. But to me, this gift was the ultimate affirmation of the trust we had built over the years, to the point that we knew one another well enough to joke around while showing respect and working well together. And if you've ever been in customer service, a joke and a few choice words are sometimes all you've got.

After that assignment, I served in another dozen leadership roles at AT&T Business until I eventually took the helm as the CEO in 2019. That leadership experience in customer service spurred much of the subsequent success I had, inspiring me to further develop and practice this new way of leading.

Leading Bigger: A More Strategic, Accurate View of Inclusive Leadership

When I first encountered the term *inclusive leadership,* sometime in the 2000s, it seemed like the perfect way to describe my philosophy: I wanted to connect all my stakeholders to the meaning and impact of our work. I sought to achieve high performance, delivering shareholder value while embracing the workforce as people first, respecting the fact that they played out their roles in the broader context of their lives and identities. Inclusive leadership is at the heart of what I call leading bigger; in fact, I often consider the two terms synonymous. How can any organization perform to its fullest if it leaves some constituents outside of a circle of belonging?

And yet, as inclusion became a priority for business, it has somehow been buried deep in the HR department, somewhere where no one would ever think to look: at the very end of the DEI (diversity, equity, and inclusion) acronym.

Ironically, *inclusion* itself has been made *too small.* In the business world, the use of the word has been focused primarily on workforce representation, with a heavy emphasis on gender, race, and physical disability.

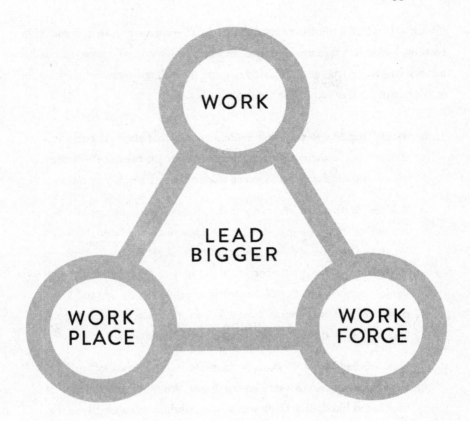

While this is important, it's certainly not complete. We need to redefine—or perhaps more accurately define—the term.

Inclusion, as I define it, is not just about people. It can also relate to the work itself, through, for instance, taking in larger datasets and more viewpoints for better decision-making. And it can encompass the workplace, more agilely addressing where, when, and how we work to support the needs of the business and its people in any given moment.

Leading bigger is where it all comes together, where the care for this "big tent" of people and the values-and-purpose-based assessment of inputs are translated into action. Leading bigger has to be driven by a compelling purpose and values, which are not platitudes, but rather lived. The goals are better decisions, improved performance, and ultimately a greater impact. Impact means you have the power to make real and enduring change for the better.

This is what I mean by leading bigger: **widening your perspective to have greater performance and impact.** How you achieve that is by advancing work that matters; developing a vital, innovative workforce; and creating a trusted, agile workplace.

1. **Work That Matters:** Bigger leaders ensure that their purpose, values, and performance metrics involve and engage the people directly affected by and interested in the work of their team/organization.

2. **A Vital, Innovative Workforce:** Bigger leaders recognize the humanity of their people, taking responsibility for how the work impacts their teams' well-being while embracing all dimensions of their identity. The leader's role has inevitably expanded to understanding what is happening in the employee's career and life—potentially at any and all times. When it comes to your people, leading bigger doesn't start and stop with the workday.

3. **Your Trusted, Agile Workplace:** Considering the future of work requires that we create a safe environment. We must stop thinking of the traditional rigid boundaries of work, such as hierarchy, location, and time. Bigger leaders champion flexibility in dynamic hybrid workplaces by embracing trust and empowerment for individuals, teams, and leaders alike.

For decades we've been urged to *think* bigger, yet no one has articulated how to *lead* bigger. Thinking bigger means envisioning new, undreamed-of possibilities that yield progressive breakthroughs; leading bigger is how you get this done. You can't think your way into market-winning growth; execution is required. High performance, innovation, and creative solutions require you to have teams who are energized and to earn the support and even friendship of the important groups that surround your company, including your customers and the communities in which you work.

In order to successfully engage with so many, the bigger leader needs to unearth and articulate a common purpose and needs to develop a new interpersonal tool kit: empathy, caring, and listening, to name just a few elements.

The upsides of this approach are indeed bigger. According to the *Harvard Business Review*—where inclusive leadership is discussed in this broader manner as embodying the traits of humility, curiosity, and active learning, rather than a more narrow DEI-based version of the term—inclusive organizations are 73 percent more likely to reap innovation revenue (i.e., sales from new products and services), 70 percent more likely to capture new markets, up to 50 percent more likely to make better decisions, and up to 36 percent more likely to have above-average profitability. And inclusive leaders create a 17 percent increase in team performance, a 29 percent increase in team collaboration, and a 76 percent decreased risk of attrition (i.e., employees leaving).

True inclusion doesn't mean adding more to leaders' plates; they're already facing burnout and exhaustion as great as anyone else's in the workforce. But leading bigger isn't yet another task or something else that one needs to do. Instead, it's a refreshing and revitalized way to approach work, the workforce, and the workplace that will not only drive success but keep leaders and their teams engaged and inspired. Leading bigger will invigorate more people with greater degrees of cohesion and connectedness. And if we want to transform and accelerate growth, it's time to lead bigger.

Evidence of Leading Bigger

This type of leadership, which aligns people to purpose and seeks to create success beyond just the bottom line, has been evolving all around us. In retrospect, we are witnessing a seminal shift toward bigger leadership.

Trillions in investment dollars have moved into conscious investments, which focus on improving the world. This includes corporate social responsibility (CSR), concern about the impact of climate change, and an eye toward how companies are run. A movement familiar to many, labeled environmental, social, and governance (ESG) programs, is going through growing pains, as the label has too often been misapplied for the purpose of marketing investment vehicles that do not deliver on the promise. Nonetheless, investor interest in backing companies that contribute positively beyond their financial results is growing.

Consider the rise of the B Corp, a for-profit company certification program that seeks to create a better kind of capitalism. One shining example of a B Corp is Patagonia, which goes from strength to strength in its effort to do nothing less than "save our home planet." Patagonia has put in place repair and reuse programs, and seeks to produce non-trendy products meant to last, in a rejection of fast fashion. It transparently publishes data on worker pay, microplastics, and other aspects of its supply chain. Its 2025 goal is to make at least half of its synthetic materials using secondary waste streams, including ocean plastic waste, bottle collection programs, and textile waste. In what I see as an effort to lead bigger, it has a stated goal to strengthen these secondary waste supply chains to enable their use by the clothing industry at large.

For more evidence that there is a will to lead bigger, reflect on how the Business Roundtable, an association of chief executive officers of leading major American companies, decided in 2019 to adopt a new statement of purpose for corporations, declaring that "companies should serve not only their shareholders [i.e., investors], but also deliver value to their customers, invest in employees, deal fairly with suppliers, and support the communities in which they operate."

Bigger leaders have been consistently elevating the business performance of their organizations while also delivering greater strategic impact for their stakeholders over the long term. I contend that, increasingly, companies do well financially when they align with stakeholders and deliver beneficial outcomes for more than just investors. This is because our world is ever more interconnected via social media and public access to data, so company behaviors are more visible than ever. Operate in ways harmful to an important community or to employee well-being, and you will set yourself up for friction and backlash that will harm your bottom line.

Yet another sign of the move toward bigger leadership is the value we're now placing on leadership behaviors like advocacy, self-awareness, servant leadership, stakeholder excellence, a philanthropic focus, vulnerability, fairness, long-term thinking, humility, and humor (often self-deprecating, or at least not typically made at the expense of others).

These types of leaders think big and deliver bigger. They are committed to delivering outstanding performance and sustainable growth while making an impact that will not only endure but remake society for the better. This is why their efforts are often seen as groundbreaking.

Consider the lead bigger characteristics demonstrated by these notable leaders:

Warren Buffett, chairperson of Berkshire Hathaway, is arguably the most successful investor of the twentieth century. His success is based on modeling an investment style that seeks to deliver value for the long term. As a bigger leader, he has also advanced philanthropy in groundbreaking ways, such as launching an initiative in which he, Bill Gates, and Mark Zuckerberg promised to give away at least half of their wealth, while encouraging others to do the same. He has generously stated time and time again that one of the reasons for his success is that he was competing against only half of the talent pool—a direct poke at the reality of gender inequity in the workplace. And he's spoken against the unfairness of how, even though he's one of the world's richest humans, he pays lower taxes than his secretary does.

Few would argue with the assertion that Alan Mulally, former president and CEO of Ford, is a bigger leader. His turnaround of Ford during the Great Recession was anchored on his "work together" principles and practices that centered around people, communication, and a clear vision. A self-proclaimed servant leader, he believes that it is an honor to serve an organization, and his deep empathy and keen awareness are legendary for bringing out the best in those around him.

Indra Nooyi, former chair and CEO of PepsiCo, revitalized the strategic direction of the company, shifting toward healthy alternatives with an intense focus on changing consumer needs. As a bigger leader, she was consistently inclusive, considering diverse perspectives and fostering a culture of respect and understanding across her organization. She is also famous for writing thank-you notes to the parents of her executives, expressing appreciation for the contribution they make and to their parents' role in raising them.

Ken Frazier, executive chairman and former CEO of Merck, is known for playing the long game, as demonstrated in his decisions to support research and development, even when it meant a short-term hit to earnings guidance. A civil rights attorney by training, he was the first CEO to step down from President Trump's American Manufacturing Council in 2017 in light of the events and commentary around the racial violence in Charlottesville. Later, he recalled in an interview that when he subsequently arrived to speak at a manufacturing plant in North Carolina, most of the manufacturing workers had their arms crossed. He said, "I respect your views. I hope you will respect mine." After he said that, he recalls that they uncrossed their arms.

Satya Nadella, chair and CEO of Microsoft, one of the most valuable companies in the world, embodies leading bigger. He speaks of empathy not as a "soft skill" but as a skill critical to innovation, since it enables the comprehension of customers' unmet needs. He has a passion for ensuring the accessibility of workplaces and products for people with disabilities, inspired by his love for his son, who had cerebral palsy and was a quadriplegic who sadly passed away in 2022.

Julie Sweet, chair and CEO of Accenture, was the first woman to lead the global professional technology services company. At a time when responding to the Israel-Hamas war has ended careers, Sweet and her management team issued a masterfully balanced and empathetic statement, as well as committed funding for humanitarian efforts. Reflective of her lead-bigger mindset, she says, "The real driver of culture (outside of good leadership) is about how it feels to come into work every day."

Simone Biles, one of the most decorated American gymnasts of all time, demonstrated her bigger leadership when, at the top of her game, she courageously prioritized her own mental health, pulling out of several events during the Tokyo Olympics in 2021. Her actions helped normalize the conversation about the importance of mental health. She has become a global role model and advocate, inspiring people across the world.

Bigger leadership has been sprouting up all around us, but these green shoots are often overshadowed by less enlightened myopic, performative, zero-sum thinking.

The Risks of Leading Small

Once you recognize the difference, you will note the disparity between small and bigger leadership everywhere you look: the business news, global politics, educational systems, and even in our local communities and neighborhoods.

Do you recognize any of these "leading small" behaviors? And more important, can you remember how these behaviors have made you *feel*? Did they affect your ability to do your job?

- **Penny-wise, pound-foolish:** Enforcing maddening budget cuts made without consideration to how they will choke long-term innovations and prospects of greater growth.

- **Narrow lens:** Myopically optimizing the performance of your own team, even when it is to the detriment of the organization.

- **Micromanaging:** Intervening to the point where your team stops learning or devising their own strategies, thus displaying a lack of trust and suppressing human ingenuity.

- **Missing the big picture:** Focusing on a single performance data point (often one that is incentivized), and thus missing the larger context of the problem you are trying to solve.

- **Self-focused:** Power-hungry, selfish, credit-stealing, and intimidating leaders who create toxic work environments that undercut growth rather than focusing on the team's spirit and the bigger picture.

- **Deflection:** Leaders who inflict crushing pressure on their employees, taking no ownership of the impossible demands they are imposing, then tell their people to meditate to manage their wellness and bring their best selves to the job.

And how about these characteristics of *bigger leaders*? Can you recall someone who exemplified these characteristics? How did you feel working with, or for, them? Did they help bring out the best in you?

- **Being a bigger person:** Demonstrating vulnerability, admitting mistakes, looking to solve conflict through respect and understanding.

- **Seeking a broader impact:** Connecting with the wider circle of people who will feel the effects of the business. Bridge-building in an attempt to find mutual benefit.

- **Scouring the horizon:** Seeking more data points and viewpoints to fill in blind spots. Identifying opportunities and potential pitfalls to guide the team confidently forward, mitigating and managing risk, for sustainable outcomes. Steering the team masterfully around the rocks.

- **Embracing the whole of your team:** Seeing each individual as having value and potential, not just in the context of their work, but in the context of their life. Working with individuals according to their unique strengths, weaknesses, and aspirations.

- **Inspirational:** Fueling a team with a shared purpose supported by a culture of belonging and the psychologically safe environments in which people can develop new ideas and display excellence.

- **Reflective:** Demonstrating self-awareness and humility, recognizing the impacts of their dispositions and behaviors on the well-being of the team. Continually learning, improving, and growing. Also, thinking deeply and systemically about a problem, identifying root causes, and devising long-term solutions.

You are not *either* a bigger leader or a small leader—we all have attributes of both. Most important, we all have the potential to lead bigger. You don't check a box and immediately become a bigger leader; it's a continuous lifelong journey you consciously choose to partake in.

Look at both lists and consider your own behaviors to date in your career. When have you led small? When were you a bigger leader?

How to Read This Book

The purpose of this book is to introduce and advance the topic of bigger leadership by reframing inclusion as an essential leadership competency applied to the work, workforce, and workplace. Each of these pillars is covered in its own section, where you'll discover strategies and practices inspired by real-world examples. To bring additional facets of inclusive leadership to life in order to widen our perspectives, I interviewed three leadership visionaries whose life's purpose and practice embody excellence. In the last section of the book, I am honored to feature one-on-one conversations with General Stanley McChrystal, Arianna Huffington, and Adam Grant. Their guidance to leaders of today and tomorrow is both inspiring and invaluable.

Making a leadership move of this magnitude isn't always easy. But leading bigger rewards both those who undertake this transformation and the people they reach. In a world of uncertainty, you'll drive lasting results while contributing to significant outcomes, having a greater impact on those you care about while delivering strong levels of performance. In a world of labor shortages and talent wars, you'll attract, engage, and retain outstanding team members who will not only contribute to your organization today but position you for success in the future. In a world of divisiveness, you'll create vital bonds with everyone connected to your business—even those whose ideologies are different from yours. And in a world where the pace of change and innovation is guaranteed to accelerate, you'll create a flexible culture along with an agile and responsive workplace—one that's distinctive because it's where the very best people, now and in the future, want to belong.

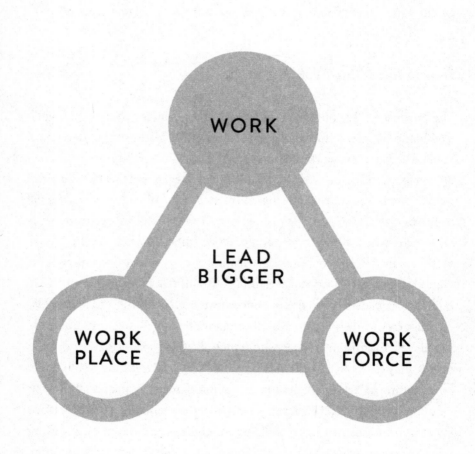

PART ONE

WORK THAT MATTERS

Bigger leaders know that work for work's sake is not an end game. Yes, the objective for a business is typically profitable growth. But even your bottom line will suffer if that's the *only* goal.

For the work to matter, begin with the *why*: your **PURPOSE.** Purpose is your reason for being. It grounds what you will do to make a difference. Clarity of purpose serves as the true north for every team, making it one of the most powerful instruments in a bigger leader's toolbox.

Next comes the *how* of your work, guided by your core and aspirational **VALUES.** Employees, customers, business partners, and even investors want to work with organizations whose values align with theirs. Bigger leaders use values to help them navigate while making tough decisions.

And finally, the ultimate goal of your work is to deliver and advance **PERFORMANCE.** Bigger leaders define performance against the impact to an intentional array of stakeholders and measure accordingly.

CHAPTER TWO

PURPOSE

BEYOND THE DAILY GRIND

Do the work to develop, harness, and evolve your purpose as your foundation for being. Without purpose, your work risks becoming meaningless or irrelevant. Your stakeholders will be uninspired, loyalty will be scarce, and the purpose-led team will outcompete you.

When my father worked for AT&T Bell Laboratories back in the day, there used to be a saying: "It's not life or death; it's dial tone." This tongue-in-cheek comment was intentionally self-limiting—likely a release valve from the pressure of work at the prestigious research facility that invented the transistor and the laser. Smart as they were, I do wonder if any of those Bell Labs folks had ever seen a classic horror film where the soon-to-be victim picks up a phone receiver only to recognize with a chilling effect that there is no dial tone. *Oh no! The line has been cut. We're doomed!*

By the time I started at AT&T in 1990, we recognized our work could *absolutely* mean life or death, and not just in the movies. A slate of real-world scenarios comes to mind: a call to the police, outreach to a mental health crisis hotline, the signal from a Life Alert device from an elderly relative. Or the ability for a hospital to summon a helicopter airlift to a better-equipped facility, with near real-time sharing of patient data to physicians when every second matters. A business's livelihood is on the line if they lose their connectivity to track inventory, serve customers, support point-of-sale systems for salespeople, process financial transactions, resolve acute issues, and more.

Our purpose, or the essential *why* behind the work we do, during much of my time at AT&T was to advance communications, or as we often said, to *create connection*. When it was time to launch my own career, having already followed in my father's footsteps by becoming an electrical engineer, I was drawn to the communications industry as an entry point due to its increasing importance as the backbone of business and of our lives. I frequently referred to our services as the lifeline for businesses—a far cry from some of the less purpose-focused mantras of the past. (In 1992, the company's slogan was "The right choice.") Between my father's era and my own, we experienced a fascinating shift in the understanding of our work's purpose.

Of course, there was purpose in the earlier days at "the telephone company." In fact, as a child visiting my father's offices at the famed Bell Laboratories facility in Holmdel, New Jersey, I could see they were engineering a marvelous tomorrow. The transistor-shaped water tower at the front of the property, which stands sixty feet tall and was built in 1961 to commemorate the invention of the transistor some fourteen years prior, looked to my young eyes like a UFO had landed. This was the 1970s, and there were no personal computers. I was struck by the reams of graph paper, the computer punch cards, and the drawings on the walls by the researchers. Even decades later, the 1993 campaign and tagline "You Will" showcased the futuristic things those scientists believed were coming: reading books online, using GPS for directions, and working from the beach—all of which are quite ordinary today.

Purpose at Bell Laboratories in that era, in my father's time, was the innovation itself—imagining and developing the technology that would ultimately underpin the internet and so much more. No doubt that purpose inspired my father and was the reason he was excited to go to the office every day. But still, it was innovation without a fully clear vision of its impact and effect on business or societal outcomes. They were living in the pure joy of innovation.

In my time at AT&T, I saw the critical purpose behind our work in networks and connection evolve. Whereas they originally served simply as pipelines for communications, they ended up driving huge transformations in our lives, in how we lived, worked, and played. By definition, connections enable inclusion: the ideas and inventions from my dad's era brought people together across distances, language barriers, socioeconomic groups, and more. Fast-forward to the modern-day world where communication and connection have become ubiquitous—and in many ways nearly as important—as the air we breathe. We felt the urgency of this purpose every day at work.

A Deceptively Obvious Bottom-Line Business Imperative

Which feels better, buying boxes of Girl Scout cookies from a troop of hopeful young service-oriented entrepreneurs in uniform outside a supermarket? Or going inside and taking some Oreos off the shelf? The Oreos are certainly less expensive. But when we support the Girl Scouts by buying cookies from them, it smacks of community service and moral gain (even beyond our love of Thin Mints or Tagalongs).

In such clear-cut cases, the advantage of purpose is obvious. But the role of purpose in business leadership is often poorly understood and undermined. Here's how:

- Many businesses run on hollow promises of purpose. (Facebook states its purpose is "to bring the world closer together," which, I suspect, a good number of its users would disagree with.)

- Some businesses do not identify a purpose at all. They likely have a mission statement that focuses on what their business does, but they fail to describe the why behind their work, thus missing an opportunity to establish a more emotional connection with the people they do business with.

- Some leaders admire purpose-driven companies—like the shoe company Toms or the apparel company Bombas, both known for their "buy one, donate one" policy—but consider them a separate kind of business that's more philanthropically minded as opposed to one committed to financial outcomes. These leaders don't see the benefit in identifying a compelling purpose for their own companies.

- Leaders who have established a clear purpose for the company at large may not always ask every team to define their own why, thus leaving much of the company ungrounded in their goals.

Purpose-driven work isn't contrary to profit-driven work. For instance, climate tech and renewable energy can create opportunities for both sustainability goals and economic growth. Delivering consistently strong financial performance does not require that you sacrifice your commitment to the community and planet. In fact, increasingly customers, investors, and other stakeholders are placing more value on whether companies are contributing to the greater good. Leading bigger means facing potentially conflicting choices in making decisions and optimizing for both short- and long-term impact: Gallup found that "a 10% improvement in employees' connection with the mission or purpose of their organization leads to an 8.1% decrease in turnover and a 4.4% increase in profitability."

This transformation shows no sign of stopping: generational changes coupled with technological advancements will continue to drive it for decades to come. Companies that don't tie to purpose in a bigger way now in their strategy, policy, and everyday operations will simply be less relevant, less competitive, and therefore less valuable.

Think of Dove soap, which has gone from a $200 million brand in the nineties to a value of $6.5 billion in 2023, making it the number one bar soap. While Dove has done much with the expansion of its product lines and merchandising, many credit its link to a purpose, focusing on countering toxic beauty standards to raise young women's self-esteem.

Compare that to its competitor Ivory, whose promise to its customers was that its soap was so pure, "It floats." It came to light over time that a bar of Ivory soap floats not due to its vaunted purity, but because of the air whipped into it in the manufacturing process. This purpose didn't connect with customers in the same way, with Ivory now the sixth soap brand, despite extending its brand to a wider product range.

Generational Considerations

Those new to the workforce are looking at a company's purpose to determine who will honor their values and their lives comprehensively. Beyond just compensation, they're assessing purpose in terms of the organization's inclusiveness and environmental impact.

Research shows us that Gen Z (those born between 1997 and 2012) is the most socially minded and diverse generation, while also being the first generation to have 24-7 access to the internet from the beginning of their lives. According to Deloitte's Global Gen Z and Millennial Survey, almost 40 percent of respondents say they've "rejected work assignments due to ethical concerns. More than a third have turned down employers that they feel aren't doing enough on matters such as the environment, DEI, or mental health." As a core group of blossoming employees, customers, community members, entrepreneurs, and investors, they're seeking more connection to purpose at work than prior generations.

Fifty percent of Gen Z identify as people of color, and 20 percent identify as LGBTQ+. Over 38 percent of Gen Z have already entered the workforce, so their influence is quickly shaping our culture. This is a group who know how to both dig for information and broadcast when they discover a disconnect. They are sharp, deeply engaged, and cynical—as they grew up exposed to a range of global to local issues such as climate change, the pandemic, the Great Recession, gun violence, and

Born	Generation
1925 1945	Silent Generation
1946 1964	Baby Boomers
1965 1980	Generation X
1981 1996	Millennials
1997 2012	Generation Z
2013 2025	Generation Alpha

an acute awareness of strife in the world, all through technologically enabled transparency in near real time. The most diverse generation that's entered the workforce to date, they want jobs that not only compensate them well but also align with their values while fitting into their desired lifestyle.

Your communications may yet be confined to in-person town halls and mass email blasts, but still require tailoring to a more technologically savvy audience who is carefully assessing whether you live up to your words. Some will criticize the overreliance of those in younger generations on smartphones, but the youngest adults among us are extremely sophisticated consumers of social media communications and marketing. Your brand's truth is always on full display.

Long story short: Gen Z will discern when you are pretending or being disingenuous, and they have the capacity to unleash a thousand memes to call you out on it.

Purpose is most engaging when it's tied to our hopes for ourselves and the world around us. Even the concept of hope itself is different for these upcoming generations as well. Simply having a job is insufficient for most. Most of Gen Z and those younger did, after all, come of age in a years-long pandemic. In America, they have no memory of the time before deep political division and the government's inability to solve key problems like mass shootings and women's access to healthcare. They may have early recollections of the housing crash. They are perhaps a little less susceptible to traditional notions of the American Dream. Hence, work that speaks to other job characteristics (like meaning, impact, connection, and growth) becomes even more important as the workplace evolves.

But is desiring meaningful work just a Gen Z priority? As a Gen Xer, I've felt most successful when I had a deeper connection to the work I did —and this connection usually manifested itself in the relationships with those around me, boosting the passion I felt for my profession. Admittedly, I didn't have this passion for every one of my seventeen different corporate jobs. But I would argue that if you ask workers of any age or tenure to remember a moment when they truly were engaged in their role, they would reference the times when they made a difference by solving problems, working with people they enjoyed while contributing to a greater good. In my very first sales job, I realized that my role was to grow the customer relationship. This meant that I had to stop selling and simply listen. I needed to understand the strategy, goals, and challenges of my customers' businesses as well as their individual client perspectives and needs. Then I could help implement solutions that could enable customers to achieve their goals. That was always deeply satisfying.

But when I felt disconnected to the purpose of the work I was doing, my engagement suffered—as did my performance. I called this stultifying feeling "boredom burnout." Different from simple burnout, when your physical and/or mental energy is depleted, boredom burnout was when I felt my capabilities and potential were severely underutilized. Imagine my surprise when I learned that there is a syndrome called "boreout," first cited in 2007. Boreout can result from many things, including the lack of intellectual challenge, the lack of purposeful work, and the monotony of the day-to-day. To power through these situations, I searched for extra-curricular activities outside of my day job to ensure that I was growing in some way. Sometimes this included getting more involved in company programs such as employee groups or training initiatives. Other times I found more enrichment externally, including volunteering in local and national nonprofits whose causes compelled me in some way. Though I supplemented my sense of fulfillment with these other activities, imagine what the organization would have gained if they had been able to harness my full capacity.

But things have significantly changed compared to when I entered the corporate environment over three decades ago. Employees in earlier eras were managed largely for efficiency. As AI and automation take on more than just rote tasks, we see an important shift: Humans increasingly need to be led in ways that support their creativity and ingenuity. Attracting and retaining talent—and keeping that talent engaged—are the challenges for modern management. Linking talent to purpose on a journey of growth is a winning and energizing mix. If you can achieve that, you'll reduce a huge amount of metaphorical friction on your path.

Identify Your Team or Organization's Stakeholders

For many organizations, shareholders (aka investors) reign supreme, and their lens on performance is very specific: They want a return on their equity and investment. There's nothing wrong with that, of course. Shareholders provide the capital that is the lifeblood of our economy. The returns on their investments also fund necessary elements of our society, such as the retirement income to everyone from teachers to police officers.

There is also a wider spectrum of *stakeholders*, including employees, your management and executive team, suppliers and partners, the community, and more. These can vary widely by organization, by the industry involved, and by your role. For example, a public university president's stakeholders would include staff, faculty, students, parents, alumni, donors, recruiting organizations, residents of the local community, and taxpayers. In certain industries, labor unions, regulators, lobbyists, and media would be considered important stakeholders. These potential stakeholders represent an illustrative example. You may not have this many, but the important thing is to define who has an interest in the existence and performance of your group and company and understand why.

Stakeholders are a collection of communities. These communities can be geographic (your town, country, or part of the world), but can also be defined by other demographic dimensions. In the workplace, there are also functional communities—for example, analysts, who track what's happening in the industry, discuss trends, and wield power and influence over key decision-makers and customers.

One of the guiding tenets of being a bigger leader is that you must resist the urge to categorize people with labels, often into binary, fixed boxes. It is absolutely possible that a single person or a group could hold different stakeholder roles. Your employees are members of the community. Your suppliers and shareholders may also be your customers. And stakeholdership itself is fluid—for example, if a privately held company goes public, the expansion of ownership broadens into a new group of investors as shareholders.

Personally, I use the word *stakeholder* (someone who has an interest in something, in this case your work) to include shareholders (any person or institution that owns at least one share in a company, also known as an investor in your business); others think these two groups work at odds. Yet a growing number of companies are doing it all: they're satisfying their shareholders and taking care of the rest of their stakeholders, including their communities and the environment.

This has sometimes been referred to as the shift from shareholder capitalism to stakeholder capitalism, the movement that recognizes that acting only to serve the financial interest of the shareholder is not enough. Your breadth of stakeholders now expect organizations to answer for their needs as well. And I would posit that being at odds with key stakeholders puts shareholder value at risk.

Even if you remain skeptical about this evolution and long for the days of focusing solely on shareholders, you must broaden your perspective, given how interconnected the world is today. If you neglect to consider a key stakeholder, it may affect your performance and potential for future growth. Take Segway as an example.

The overhyped introduction of Segway into the market in the early 2000s represented an exciting, albeit bulky, new mode of personal transportation. However, the corporation failed to consider the practical reality of city infrastructures, localized policies, and safety requirements before they launched—neglected stakeholders on all sides, including city planners and other officials, residents, pedestrians, and more. Had they been involved in the early planning, the outcome could have been different. Instead, with Segway's high-profile accidents and bans from cities, their sales were doomed from the start, and after a series of changes in ownership, production stopped in 2020.

And now we see a similar pattern with the overnight scooter drops in various cities (in which companies leave paid scooters all over a city, without helmets, to the alarm of public safety officials). Here we see again that misalignments with stakeholders and purpose can take your company down: Electric scooter maker Bird, once valued at $2.5 billion, filed for bankruptcy in late 2023. The company operated a short-term scooter rental business in 350 cities, but reported losses as problems surfaced, including emergency rooms reporting surging injuries related to use of the products, and scooter bans in some cities.

E-bikes, while certainly not injury free, are capturing much of the promise originally exhibited by Segway and scooters through better community connection and advocacy, and by plugging into existing bike etiquette and infrastructure. Cities and state governments across the country, themselves looking to reduce traffic and emissions, have established rebates and tax credits that subsidize purchases of e-bikes. And in some cases, officials are finding that creating armies of new cyclists can then in turn create citizen support for further improving infrastructure such as bike lanes. The e-bike market is predicted to grow to over $119 billion by 2030.

Words to Work By: The Purpose Statement

Okay, sure. It helps to have a purpose, and one that matters to your stakeholders. But how do you define it, exactly?

Let's say you lead a team where the why is simply not clear. No Girl Scouts. No life-or-death concerns. Perhaps you sell chairs. How do you surface your why? What purpose will sustain you and your people through a commute in bad weather, or after your baby kept you up half the night?

Here's how IKEA tied their work of "selling furniture and home goods" to their purpose statement: "To offer a wide range of well-designed, functional home furnishing products at prices so low that as many people as possible will be able to afford them." By building an intentional purpose statement, IKEA underlines its contribution to society and lives up to it through their selections. Sure, you might have an empathetic ache in your back when you imagine "as many people as possible" sitting on the floors of their homes wriggling together flat-pack furniture with tiny Allen wrenches. But you can certainly agree that IKEA is affordable and functional, serving their purpose of clean, thoughtful design for the masses. College students, families, and startup founders can access aesthetically pleasing furnishings at prices that are within their reach, meeting a real need in society.

To access this deeper meaning, I've found it helpful to go beyond the focus on *what* you're doing. Ask yourself and each other: *Why? Why you?* What makes your *how* the optimal choice and different from current or future competitors in the market?

No matter the size of your team or the work you're doing, you're on a mission to reach a destination, realize your vision, and achieve your desired outcomes. If you're still struggling to express what you do differently, ask yourself, *What if we didn't exist? Who would care? And why?*

In my early roles, before I had team leadership responsibilities, I learned to greatly value those bosses who explained the context for our work, within the broader why of the company. I strove to emulate them by creating localized purpose statements for my teams that would "ladder up" to the company's vision. My very first boss at AT&T was one of my best, and she set the foundation for me of what *bigger* meant. I was an engineer focused on the billing architecture of AT&T's network. She showed us how our work was used, took us on field trips to service centers that benefited from our projects, and constantly talked to us about the positive impact of our contributions to customers. Her approach was people-centric—from us as her employees, to our colleagues that we helped, to the customers we served. I became what I would come to call a "context gal" in that first role, constantly seeking to connect across the what, who, how, and why.

When I led a product management team, I'd highlight our customers' pain points, to underline our company's purpose: that we needed to constantly innovate. Then I tied this to the quantitative growth of the company in revenue, margin, and market share. Our ability to develop and launch new products could both serve existing customers and win new ones—and that was at the heart of growing the business. And our focus wasn't just on the products themselves but on how our customers would experience them.

Bigger leaders are dealers in hope, and a primary objective I always had when speaking with my team was affirming to them how important their roles were to the greater good—to show them that they really mattered and give them a sense of how their efforts contributed to the current and future growth of our company.

To truly inspire people, you must choose your words intentionally when expressing purpose. While your statements should be aspirational and ambitious, you also want them to be attainable and actionable. Credibility is key. Oftentimes companies choose words that feel too lofty, abstract, broad, or buzzy, and the effect is like an astrological horoscope that is generically applicable but says nothing.

Ultimately it doesn't matter what words you choose if your stakeholders can't envision what you're seeking to create. Certainly, Steve Jobs's brain was afire with futuristic notions of how technology would change our lives. But he kept Apple's mission simple so that we mere mortals could keep up: "To make a contribution to the world by making tools for the mind that advance humankind." Note the reference to "tools for the mind"—he was careful not to limit it to "computers"—even though the rest of us had never yet seen an iPod or an app store.

Let's assess a few examples of companies who have made an explicit effort to be bigger and inclusive in their approach to their purpose:

Nike's vision is to "bring inspiration and innovation to every athlete* in the world," with an asterisk that "*if you have a body, you're an athlete." That's an ultimate statement of inclusion and leading bigger: *Everyone* is or can be an athlete. As a sporting apparel and gear company, they could reasonably have stated that their purpose was "to create groundbreaking sports innovation," but they didn't just focus on their customers. They included the many more stakeholders affected by their business: "to create groundbreaking sports innovations, make our products sustainably, build a creative and diverse global team, and make a positive impact in the communities in which we live and work." The brand goes big here, asserting who they are, what they want to represent, and who they serve. Do they need to say both "groundbreaking" and "innovations"? Is that perhaps redundant? We can nitpick. But in all, the statement lays the groundwork for customers and employees alike to strengthen their connection to the brand.

Let's look at an unexpected business-to-business (B2B) example, Old Dominion Freight Line. You might expect a trucking and logistics company to settle on something like "We deliver on time, every time," and while that would be sufficient, it would miss out on the potential of purpose statements to compel stakeholders to join them. I love the tagline they actually have emblazoned on their trucks: "Helping the world keep promises." As you peel back what they do and more fully understand the how and why, you can appreciate their focus on dependability and the power of promises. They chose words that create meaningful connection and a visceral emotional bond to not just their partners or businesses, but the end customer as well. In just five words, Old Dominion captured the beating heart of their why.

The point is that you should strive to be conscious about the power behind your purpose statement, choosing language that embodies the work and the people you want to feel included in it. Your commitment should directly inform your choices about people, products, processes, and platforms.

Connecting People to Your Purpose

In many of my leadership roles over the years, I've tailored my feedback to my work group, using precise examples of what we were responsible for, pushing them to envision how their contributions yield certain business results and outcomes for the company.

At AT&T, we actively integrated customers into our leadership gatherings by having them speak at summits or kickoffs about how we supported them. Once, the CEO and chief information officer (CIO) of a leading nationwide hospice provider described how our 5G mobile solutions enabled them to create virtual reality experiences for their patients, which reduced pain levels from a 10 to a 2 in some patients and provided bucket-list virtual experiences for others. These stories gave me goose bumps and pushed me to engage customers even earlier in our product strategy and launch processes.

We brought in clients regularly as part of our customer advisory councils focused on particular industries, technologies, or transformation objectives. As examples, we discussed how important communication solutions were for support groups such as first responders, whose mission was to protect and save lives, and how the diversification of customer networks across all industries intensified the need for an even more aggressive approach to cybersecurity. Much of our conversation was spent on the customer experience, and oftentimes their candor was sobering. Hearing valued customers tell us when we'd failed them was uncomfortable but necessary. But then again, their reinforcement of how important we were to them as a key partner reminded us that their constant contributions made us better.

Across the country, a key focus for AT&T was to help bridge the digital divide, especially with access to educational experiences. We partnered with local organizations, including schools and nonprofits, to create centers that provided connectivity for underserved communities. For instance, we saw that our Connected Learning Centers did more than just give access to the internet. Students of all ages were able to complete their homework assignments, families were able to bond more readily with new games and learning activities, and patient volunteers made sure senior citizens were kept current with new technology. This enabled a higher level of multigenerational camaraderie in local communities, which was tremendously powerful. Through these local partnerships, which are still ongoing, AT&T has a tangible impact by helping people thrive better in our digital world. Though it's important to keep in mind that boasting about your company's community actions and goodwill might be perceived as performative, bringing those you touch to life through storytelling and with insight from real people clarifies your purpose.

Bigger leaders give those around them *reasons to believe*.

Safety Tips

Be aware of a few things to watch out for when creating a purpose statement for your team and organization. The first and most common mistake is to try to PR your way through it. You cannot. This is not an exercise in marketing, HR, or advertising. It's the work of leadership, culture, policies, and practices. I once heard it said that your purpose must be embodied "on the walls and in the halls." Your leadership behaviors, decisions, and operating practices must harmonize.

Next, be clear about your circle of control. Bigger leaders focus on the whole ecosystem of other team members, even those who may not be inside their organization. I've always had my PR, HR, legal, and financial teams at my side. Their leaders were in every staff meeting, and their teams at every kickoff. Despite the fact that in the hierarchy of the company, they reported to corporate, they were integral members of the team, dedicated to the same purpose and results. We operated as one unit, and my leaders and I strived to treat them as such. This is also how I approached key partners outside of the company, whether in product or channel roles.

This is another hallmark of leading bigger: functional inclusion. Functional inclusion means inviting participation beyond your immediate purview—reaching out to the legal team, the admins, the interns, the IT staff, and more. As a leader, you can't succeed if you're focused only on the people in your direct chain of command or even just in your company. To fully deliver on your organization's purpose, you need the involvement of others. If your IT support team doesn't know the purpose or the priorities of your organization, they might run a system update on a deadline day. Or if your legal team doesn't know the purpose, they might allocate resources to a thick compliance process that could slow down your most urgent efforts. This is all to say that you must embrace inclusivity to elevate your strategy, planning, and execution. If your domain is technology, does your outlook include customer application, innovation, and competitive positioning? If your group is responsible for communications, does your focus go beyond speaking to the organization's products and services to also include publicizing its diversity of talent, active presence in the community, or contributions to global priorities such as climate change? In fact, as you refine your purpose statement, asking people outside of your typical realm of influence for input is a must to make sure that what you come up with is big (aka inclusive) enough.

Purpose: A Gift for Your Brand Team

The days are long gone when a company owned its brand's perception. In the noisy social media and meme-driven communications world today, you no longer control the megaphone. Your people's and thus your brand's actual behaviors will speak louder than any slogan.

This "brand truth" needs to come first. Asking your marketing team to tack on some inauthentic purpose in an advertising campaign is sending them on a fool's errand; any daylight between the slogan and reality will make your company a target of ridicule, at best.

At worst, a vocal subset can co-opt your brand for a variety of reasons. Wolf packs can swoop in to take your brand down because it serves some other orthogonal purpose in the culture wars or identity politics. In the investing world, meme stock traders can decide to pump up or crash your stock price, almost on a whim. And whether the dustup is warranted or entirely random almost doesn't matter, because it's now your business's reality to face and deal with in the marketplace of ideas. In any case, a thoughtful brand promise is ballast for your brand ship on the stormy seas of modern brand management.

This is why leading bigger is not just some new management trend, but a leadership imperative. If your efforts rally a wider stakeholder group around a purpose, you are creating durable brand value. Do this well and you may see your own wolf pack emerge and defend you when issues arise. According to research by advertising firm Porter Novelli, "Americans are willing to go out on a limb to support their favorite purpose-driven brands. Seventy-three percent of Americans say they would likely defend a purpose-driven company if someone spoke poorly of it, and another 67 percent say if that company made a misstep, they would be more willing to forgive it over a company that did not lead with purpose. In this way, purpose not only helps create relationships that transcend transactions, but also future-proofs brands by attracting loyal consumers that will stick with them through good times and bad."

However, this cannot be taken lightly or for granted: Once a purpose has been communicated, a promise has been made.

Your marketing teams will have much to do: They must be empowered to broadcast and disseminate your messages, and also to listen and report back. They'll be able to spot where you're falling short on your promises or where your purpose needs a refresh in a changing market. Create that collaboration by being curious, asking questions, and reviewing the data together. Invite your marketing experts to provide feedback on areas where your promise falls short; they need to know you will listen and not shoot the messenger.

At AT&T, our business customers and distributors told us they didn't see themselves in our strategy and purpose, because our advertising and messaging focused heavily on the consumer market. We were also getting this feedback from our own people who served businesses. These employees yearned to see their work reflected in the company's external communications and were starting to wonder if their contributions even mattered to the company.

At the highest level, the company had two customer markets they served: consumers (business to consumer, or B2C) and businesses (business to business, or B2B). While our business customers were fewer in number than our consumer customers, they were equally important to our operations. Our B2B organization served businesses of all sizes and the public sector, including the federal government, the military, and educational and healthcare institutions. These diverse clients didn't relate to our consumer messaging, though of course in some cases, they were also individual consumers of AT&T's services. But to position ourselves as their provider of choice, we had to understand what they were looking for beyond the typical consumer lens, namely a cool product at a competitive price.

We didn't alter our consumer marketing, which was heavily centered on value and ease. ("Buy one, get one free, on our most popular smartphones!") Consumer messaging was meant to be simple. Businesses, on the other hand, were swimming in complexity, and they needed to hear that we understood. So we spoke to the problems of businesses, who often had hundreds of suppliers and needed to be open to direct communications with all of them, while still staying safe from cyberattacks. This message was not a simple one, and we used the tagline "the power of &" because businesses needed security *and* agility *and* reliability *and* scalability and . . . and . . . and. They wanted us to bring them expertise across technologies such as fiber and wireless, and security coupled with innovation they didn't have. They expected more support and resources than they received for their personal phone or internet services. Repeatedly, they told us our networks and connections were not just the *pipeline* for their business, but the *lifeline*. So we had to develop business messaging that reflected this. Seemingly overnight the "&" became a physical and digital symbol of who we were and what we could do for them.

As examples, we showed how our solutions could make their manufacturing lines more efficient, how they could keep their trading floors up and running, and how they could manage spikes in retail demand across both in person and online.

Not only did this messaging show up in our ads, our marketing materials, and our sales force training, but it guided the next steps in our growth transformation. We improved our operating model. We restructured our business around the market segments of Public Sector, Wholesale, Small Business and Mid Markets, and Enterprise. We aligned our sales and marketing teams to industries, so customers would be served by experts who would understand how to apply our technologies in their particular industry. Instead of just participating in their trade shows—manufacturing, financial services, retail, healthcare, and so on—we led the discussion on innovation. We eliminated silos in our customer service team to reduce frustrating handoffs. These tangible changes improved the perception and confidence not only of our customers and partners but also of our own people. New and tenured employees alike proudly donned freshly branded attire embroidered with "AT&T Business." This did wonders for our culture—and it didn't require spending tons of money doing research with consultants and agencies. We simply listened to our key stakeholders and connected the dots.

The establishment of AT&T Business went far beyond branding—it transformed the approach to our work, workforce, and workplace. This was more than an important move for our company—it was an industry first. Can you imagine the confidence we felt when, one after another, our competitors followed suit by putting "Business" after their name? Most communications organizations now have explicit sub-brands to serve businesses and operating groups. Leading bigger not only helped our organization have a greater impact for *our* customers and shareholders, but fueled changes across the entire industry, accelerating the innovation and investment focused on the business marketplace.

Bigger leaders can set up mechanisms that provide a kind of early warning system, like the customer advisory councils and supplier governance groups. Ours made us aware of gaps in serving them, encouraged us to pursue innovations that would meet their needs into the future, and affirmed when our actions were hitting the mark.

Encourage all your teams, especially those who face off to customers and other key stakeholders, to tell you the truth about shortfalls and help you diagnose any detachments. Be brave enough to address problems that arise, even if they originate from the very top of your organization.

A company founder or senior leader can be the worst offender in taking a brand into a disappointing turn. Think about Chip Wilson, the founder of Lululemon, who made comments about larger women's bodies as his defense for poor product quality in one of its lines of leggings. He resigned in 2013, after delivering a video apology derided by media commentators as "the worst apology ever." In 2024, he courted controversy again, taking aim at Lululemon for their "whole diversity and inclusion thing," saying the brand was trying to be all things to all people, and "you've got to be clear that you don't want certain customers coming in." Lululemon put out a statement distancing itself from the founder, who still holds the majority of Lululemon's shares, valued at $4 billion—a point noted in coverage of some public calls for boycotts of the brand.

Or when Greg Glassman, the founder of CrossFit, resigned two days after making comments about the Black Lives Matter movement that caused many CrossFit franchise owners to drop, or threaten to drop, the CrossFit name.

These headline-making brand missteps represent the extreme downside. There is just as much to be gained when brand messaging is strongly tied to a purpose. Ultimately, a genuine purpose creates brand superfans who provide testimonials and a community that keeps your employees engaged and excited. By crafting a purpose statement, you'll have done much of the work that will underpin your brand messaging, making your marketing efforts more efficient, effective, and authentic.

Lead Bigger Through Purpose

- Do you know what impact your company makes in the world? This is more than what you sell. What problem do you solve? What does your team uniquely contribute? Why does it *matter*?

- Do your employees and customers believe your company embodies your purpose?

- Do you have systems to measure your ability to fulfill your purpose?

- Does each team have its own purpose statement that supports and enhances the company's purpose?

- Do you have a plan to refresh your purpose as the market changes and circumstances warrant?

CHAPTER THREE

VALUES

ALIGN PRINCIPLES WITH BEHAVIOR

Like purpose, creating company values can often be an exercise in spinning platitudes. Big values resonate deeply with your stakeholders, often both professionally and personally—but only if your leaders and every member of your team live them.

In sales, one of the things they teach you is that "The customer's perception is your reality."

I can tell you: That adage works—until the moment it doesn't.

In my case, this happened when I was running a sales organization, and we were trying to retain the business of a disgruntled client.

My team tried addressing the client's long-standing pain points, which included chronic billing issues and inconsistent communications with people who were no longer part of the group. We tried to address the problems with enthusiasm and win a fresh start, something we called "taking 'em through the car wash." But somehow our effort wasn't paying off as it usually would; we weren't turning the situation around. The team asked if I could join a call with the customer's CIO, who was their executive decision-maker.

After brief introductions, I started off the conversation by saying, "I know we've disappointed you in the past with billing and service issues. Your dissatisfaction with our responsiveness is absolutely valid. We take ownership of this, and I commit to you to remedy these issues with our new team, including my personal support." It didn't take long on the phone with this CIO for me to see what was happening. I was confronted with a wall of f-bombs and even a phrase I had to look up afterwards to know if I should feel offended. (He claimed, "You slipped me a mickey," in an accusation that somehow we had been deceiving him all along.) After his rant, I said calmly, "I respect how you feel about these experiences, and I assure you that this is not the way we strive to do business. We will work hard to rebuild your trust." After the team call, I scheduled another call with him one-on-one. His behavior was just as egregious during the second conversation. Despite my best efforts to assuage him, it became clear that he relished aggressively slinging allegations and uttering profanity.

Of course we valued the customer and their business. But I had to help my team understand that we had an even higher value of respect for one another, and we weren't going to further expose ourselves to abuse in attempts to sustain a relationship that was clearly toxic.

In yet another call with the CIO, I said, "We're committed to serving you and appreciate you as a customer. Over the past many months, we've worked hard to resolve prior issues. It may not be visible to you, but we're working tirelessly to address everything you're throwing at us and want to regain your confidence. But I just cannot allow the continued berating of my team. And at this point, it's not clear to me that rebuilding this relationship and our trust with each other is a priority to you." I paused, giving him an opportunity to respond. All he said was "Go on," and my impression was that he was shocked that someone was pushing back at him—because after all, he was the client. I said, "We'll continue to do our best, and we're absolutely confident that our proposal to move forward is best suited to meet the growth needs of your business. If you believe that, too, I'd ask that you refrain from verbally abusing my team.

If there is to be success going forward, I expect the common courtesy of professionalism as part of our partnership." There was an uncomfortable pause, and I could sense he wanted to lash back out as always. But he didn't. So I wrapped up the call, taking the high road of bigger leadership.

That client and the revenue associated with the company he represented evaporated. It was difficult and it hurt; I won't deny it. Walking away meant that it'd be that much harder to make our numbers that year. But it simply wasn't worth it.

In the moment, we felt like we had failed. But I had to help my team see that taking the higher road was the right one—nothing was worth that kind of irrational abuse. This CIO was fired months later. I'm not sure of the details, but I can only imagine.

Neither our company handbook nor our corporate policies had any instructions for such a situation. But what made the decision clear was a non-negotiable value: the care for the respect and psychological safety of the people on our team.

You've likely heard management consultant Peter Drucker's famous adage that culture eats strategy for breakfast. Culture is absolutely strategic, and it begins with values.

Culture is the behavioral norms exhibited by the people in any group. Leaders often find it straightforward to express their company's values through their products, services, and/or customer experience. But culture is foundational to any business's strategy; most of the time, a company's strategy is built directly off of its culture. A business's culture is expressed directly through a company's organizational values and behaviors—stated or not.

Like inclusivity, culture is not something to delegate to HR as an initiative or project. It's not a beer tap in the kitchen. It's not the tricycle races in the halls you plan at the holiday party. It is embodied by the words, habits, practices, and actions of your people, especially your leaders, demonstrated in both the best and the worst of times. Creating, sustaining, and evolving culture is at the core of bigger leadership.

As with purpose, every leader must embody professional values in both words and actions. I learned this mid-career. Tasked with facilitating a multiday strategy session with some very senior executives, I prepared for weeks without much input or guidance from my manager (despite asking for support and feedback) and headed into the first day with confidence. I was getting positive responses from the participants and thought it was coming together well. Despite the good reception, my manager asked that we meet alone early before the meetings started on the second day, then proceeded to give me devastating and less than constructive feedback. In the wee hours of the morning, I got a confidence-shattering tongue-lashing that made me question my own worthiness at the company and left me in shock.

At the time I didn't know what had hit me. Despite feeling extremely shaken, I managed to make it through the second day. After the session was over—having successfully completed our business objectives—I went into survival mode, realizing that there was no path forward so long as I reported to this manager; I had to exit stage left. After confiding my distress to some colleagues, I discovered that what happened to me was not unique. I considered leaving the company altogether, but thankfully I realized that my disconnect was with the person and not with my company. In hindsight, this experience forced me to reflect deeply on the importance of my own values and acknowledge that my time with the company would endure far beyond one challenging relationship.

This is where defining values really matters. This manager may not have been fully conscious of their compulsion to tear down the confidence of their team members. They may have even felt they were putting their people through their paces, perhaps having experienced similar treatment during their own career. But if they had focused on behaving in ways that reflected our company's values, they would have been able to rise above these unhelpful reflexes and would have become a better leader.

Since then, I vowed to myself that with every opportunity to lead people, I would embrace my values no matter the context—and I would do this through action. This "challenging boss" experience reaffirmed several core values for me: authenticity, courage, caring, and adaptability. It showed me the negative effects of a poor culture, one in which you could verbally lash out at people and treat them with a fundamental lack of respect. I also learned the value of integrity: that no matter what values might be touted, none of them made a difference if the leader acted in ways contrary to them.

Values become an important commonality as you work with stakeholders. Articulating your values *inclusively* means that you consider the expectations of your customers, staff, investors, shareholders, partners, distributors, and communities. Assess the areas you're selling your products or services in, beyond the corporate campus or the windows in your Zoom screens. Some may recall the surge of anti-Asian hate crimes from 2019 through 2021. In New York City, family and friends told me about the degree of fear in their community, especially concerning the use of public transit; it created anxiety about how to even get to and from work. And yet that concern was not sinking into the mainstream consciousness of non-Asian managers and CEOs as an issue to be addressed. If your company values safety (and I hope this would be the case!), you must be sensitive to threats outside of your personal bubble.

When it comes to establishing your values, the most important constituent to cater to is your workforce. Your company's values will have an impact on recruiting and retaining top talent and will establish a foundation for inclusive collaboration. Those selfsame values will also help clarify your position, as it did for me when faced with an abusive customer, if you're ever forced to choose between different options, such as the well-being of your people and the pursuit of a particular opportunity for revenue.

Catalyzed by the tumultuous events of the early 2020s and the soul-searching that followed, people want to work for an organization and a team whose values closely match their own. Your people now expect those values to go beyond basic leadership competencies like teamwork, collaboration, or continuous improvement. These should also reflect your social and moral priorities, such as diversity, sustainability, and a positive impact on communities. Your priorities and your values will demonstrate that you care, which is inclusion in practice. If you're uncomfortable with that idea, the alternative is to watch your talent slip away to organizations who leverage their cultural and competitive advantages. Nearly 30 percent of millennials (a massive cohort that now includes mid-career professionals) are "planning to leave their company within a year because their company doesn't match their values," according to EY research. Gen Z increasingly expects their employers to back up their values with genuine action, and I suspect Gen Alpha, children born between 2013 and 2025, will only expand that desire, given the rise in youth activism on elementary and middle school campuses. Twenty percent of Gen Alpha kids have already attended their first protest.

This isn't about virtue signaling: Research shows that values alignment increases job satisfaction, collaboration, communication, and trust while reducing turnover. Each person's own values have both personal and professional dimensions to them. Professional values could include autonomy, flexibility, stability, growth, and pay potential. Personal values could include integrity, contribution toward the greater good, balance, boundaries, transparency, and more. Your people are complex and interdependent beings. Leading bigger means taking in their wider concerns and interests with both respect and discernment.

Some managers long for the past ways of work rather than meeting the needs of a workforce that has been transformed by some generational or worldly change. But bigger leaders must wade into uncharted waters more often than not. Think of how Coca-Cola and Delta, both headquartered in Georgia, were pressed to release statements in 2021, citing their values to condemn new voter rules passed by the state legislature. The proposed rules required ID for absentee ballot requests, rather than a signature match; reduced the number of ballot drop boxes; and banned anyone from providing food or water to voters waiting in lines. Ed Bastian, the chief executive of Delta—which holds honesty as a core value—said the rules changes were based on the lie that there was widespread voter fraud in the 2020 elections in Georgia. As the largest employer of Black Americans in the state of Georgia, Bastian said he needed to be the voice of his employees, who felt targeted by the rules.

Uncertainty and division characterize much of the world—from the economy to geopolitics to national politics to the impact of emerging technologies like artificial intelligence. This dynamic landscape reinforces the need for clear values to guide your way on when to take a stand or stand down.

The Two Types of Values

Though values already exist in every organization, they may not always be conveyed clearly or meaningfully. As a bigger leader, you can frame your values in two ways. The first is through *core values,* the fundamental beliefs that drive your internal ethics. I've always called them guiding principles—what a business should base its priorities on. Core values shape the underlying behavior of the people—that is to say, the culture. Some of the most common core values that businesses cite are integrity, teamwork, respect, leadership, innovation, and focus on the customer.

The second is through *aspirational values.* Your task is to identify the core values your business revolves around, but if those current core values are insufficient to get you where you need to go or if your desired values are currently not your practiced values, it's important to set aspirational ones as guideposts for behavioral change. Perhaps you want to drive improvement in an area of your business, but you couldn't invest in it while you divested assets. Your organization might not currently embody "continuous improvement," but it's where you want to go. In that case, I recommend you set it as an aspirational value and begin to incorporate that ideal in how you work.

To bring your values to life, express them as statements, action-oriented sentences that are more comprehensive than a single word like *trust* or *integrity.* Below are some examples to jump-start your thinking:

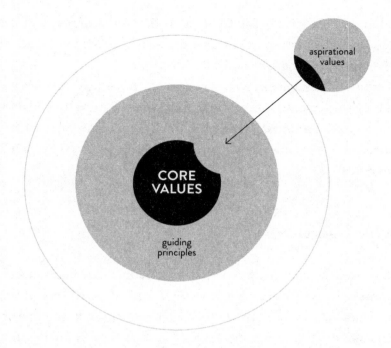

- We lead with humility.

- We trust each other, our partners, and our customers.

- We take accountability.

- We make a difference in our customers' lives.

- We fight for freedom.

- We are lifelong learners.

- We bring families together and make communities stronger.

- We make the ethical choice every time.

- We respect the whole person.

- We choose humility.

- We help every student see their full potential.

- We never settle.

- We have the highest quality products in the marketplace.

- We seek simplicity whenever possible.

- We operate sustainably for today and tomorrow.

- We bring beauty to the world.

Sometimes a value can benefit from being qualified, to ensure that the boundaries of the value are clear, or when there's some competing concern. These can show up as compound value statements, often balancing two parts that hold tension between them:

- We take our role seriously but not ourselves too seriously.

- We have the highest performance standards and give each other grace.

- We challenge convention and take smart risks.

- We demonstrate empathy and tell the truth.

Bigger leaders acknowledge that values are not static and are meant to evolve over time with your business. But be sure these changes are intentional. This also applies to you as the lead person. Being part of the evolution of a team, organization, or company shapes you as a leader—just as you shape it. Neither will "just happen." Bigger leaders catalyze the transformation of their teams by constantly seeking out more perspectives and possibilities in the interest of growth.

Negative Values: The Toxic Workplace

Negative values in an organization are characterized by toxic behaviors that are often camouflaged. No one emblazons on their walls or onboarding slides such statements as *We will assassinate your character as soon as you are out of earshot*, or *You will never pin it on me!* Yet sadly, these are the unspoken values in many workplaces: manipulation, arrogance, disrespect, gossip, bullying, bad politics, dishonesty, ruthlessness, favoritism, or discrimination—values that harm people.

The dissonance between *stated* versus *lived* values creates deep fissures in an organization or team, weakening and destroying the trust needed between leaders and their people. This disparity can be caused by just a handful of toxic people who are allowed to behave in ways that contradict the company's guiding principles. When this happens, skepticism and frustration rise while engagement and satisfaction decrease among staff and leaders who *are* walking the talk.

Bigger leaders can stop negative values from emerging by openly discussing the circumstances when negative behaviors arise. Throughout my career, I have found that many leaders focus primarily on reaffirming positive values, as opposed to speaking explicitly about the ramifications of negative values. This lopsided approach is risky. In contrast, bigger leaders have the courage to admit and cite situations when they themselves fall short of fully embodying their values. By showing their vulnerability, they create a safe place for their teams to do the same and learn from the experience.

I remember vividly the first time I did this to one of my team members. In fact, it was during my earliest experience as a manager, having a handful of people directly report to me. A member of my team had recently gotten engaged and was heavily focused on wedding planning. While she did her job well, I perceived that she was not as committed because she was not as available outside the boundaries of a standard workday. And while I thought I was a person whose core values included caring, my treatment of her at times was unfair and unrealistic because I expected her to check voice mails and emails around the clock, simply because that's what I did. After a period of several weeks, she asked for a private discussion, in which she told me how unhappy she was and that she wanted to start looking for another role. I was shocked. As she described her reasoning, I realized that the problem was my unrealistic and insensitive expectations. I apologized. We worked through a different approach that required more flexibility and respect on my end. Appropriately so. Bigger leaders own their mistakes and learn from them, especially when it comes to people. This mindset requires vulnerability and growth, leading to even more opportunities for a greater leadership impact.

None of us are perfect, not even those of us striving to be bigger leaders. When I was too quick to judge a situation, too impatient to listen to a fulsome analysis my team had done, I had to fess up to my poor behavior and apologize. These actions, no matter the cause, were contrary to our fundamental value of respect. Bigger leaders must call out these behaviors, especially in regard to their own actions.

Setting Your Organizational Values

Professors Paul Ingram and Yoonjin Choi write:

> All too often leaders assume that if they continually recite their organization's values, the words will take on an incantatory power, and employees will fall under their spell, almost like zombies. . . . [This] approach tends to have an alienating effect. No matter where people work, they don't want values imposed on them unilaterally, especially if those values don't align with their own. When that happens, they feel robbed of agency, and they become cynical.

Whether you're a new leader or one whose role sits deeper within the organization, you may not believe you need to go through a values exercise. Your organization likely has documented values, but they often exist at a very senior level and feel distant from the front line. No matter what level your work group is, the following values-setting exercise is the first step to fostering ownership of values and accountability for them within your team. Your objective is to establish localized team values that build up to the organizational expectations in a way your people can relate to and understand. For example, suppose a company's goal is to "prioritize the customer experience," and your work group is responsible for fixing the service when it breaks and resolving customer troubles. Perhaps one of your values would be to have a high-quality, rapid customer response. This value can help you decide to invest in the latest AI-powered solutions, which could provide near-real-time answers to customers' basic questions while helping guide your service representative to a customer's history more effectively and efficiently.

Instead of deciding core and aspirational values in a vacuum, bigger leaders establish organizational values with participation from a range of people. Here's the process I use:

1. Ask stakeholders to brainstorm individually.

2. Gather stakeholders for a group discussion.

3. Synthesize the results as the leader.

4. Gut-check your decision against reality.

5. Measure behaviors against your values.

6. Review and update your values and metrics regularly.

1. *Ask stakeholders to brainstorm individually.* Start by gathering a diverse group of people based on tenure, function, demographic concerns, experiences, and/or personality style. I would not recommend asking for volunteers, which tends to result in an over-abundance of extroverts when you want to hear many voices in this process. If for some reason your work group is small, reach out to your internal and external partners, such as distributors, resellers, volunteers, funders, suppliers, and even your customers.

Traditional approaches to brainstorming can yield groupthink and skew to the loudest voices in the room. To ensure that all participants have an equal footing, ask each person to write down three to five values they believe the organization stands for. Only then should you bring the group together.

2. ***Gather stakeholders for a group discussion.*** Share individual feedback and look for natural points of consolidation. Sticky notes—real or virtual—work well in enabling you to organize ideas into categories. As an example, you might group comments like "We do what we say," "We always tell the truth," or "Trust is a basis for our services and our leadership" into a common theme of integrity.

    Then give each person a certain number of votes, depending on the size of your group, and ask them to prioritize their top values. At that point, take a step back and work this process iteratively. You will see recurrent themes emerge, which in addition to integrity could include accountability, operational excellence, innovation, teamwork, customer service, and sustainability.

3. ***Synthesize the results as the leader.*** You should work to thoughtfully engage each person and to ensure agency and accountability. This is an inclusive process. However, this doesn't mean that every person has veto power at the end. As the leader, you are the one who ultimately decides which values best embody your culture and vision. Collaboration, however, is necessary for coming up with your values in an inclusive fashion.

    Once you've solicited the team's input, you can draw on marketing, PR, or communications specialists to refine the language, so your final short list is action-oriented and transparent.

4. ***Gut-check your decision against reality.*** Organizations and companies often fail to do a gut check of whether they're actually living those values. Are the values legitimate? Are you hitting all the touch points relating to a particular one? Can you think of areas in the company that aren't optimizing them efficiently? Do your people, products, services, and customer experiences embody your values? At this step, I've gathered a completely different sample of stakeholders—for example, other functional groups you work with or customer-facing teams, especially if yours is not—and asked them to evaluate how well we're living these values. Employee resource groups can be very helpful here.

Line up your set of values against your company's actual practices, processes, and policies. You may find that some of your values are actually aspirational, as discussed earlier in this chapter. It's not that you don't want to be there, it's just that you're not there yet. But there's a difference between aspirational values and values you simply aren't living up to (a sign of small leadership), which usually shows up in data and performance over time. Watch for red flags such as:

- One of your values is to have the highest-performing workforce in the industry, but your revenue-to-employee ratio and customer satisfaction scores are trending downward, falling far short of best-in-class companies.

- You want to embrace a culture of trust and transparency, but your workplace is rife with gossip, conflict, and competition.

- Your value is to lead with innovation, but your research and development (R&D) investments in head count and capital have been declining for years.

- You tell the market you provide the fastest, most reliable service, but your delivery and repair response times are slow, and you're not equipped with enough technology to improve them.

- You are committed to diversity, but your executive team and board are homogeneous. Neither reflect your targeted market or the demographics of the broader industry and environment.

5. *Measure behaviors against your values.* If you don't have a system that presents a scorecard on how you are behaving, that value isn't actually a core value, because you can't evaluate it. Certainly you can retain that guiding principle as a value, but perhaps it's better designated as an aspirational one. As an example, if you cite that one of your core values is customer focus, are you measuring all aspects of the customer experience, not only with your products and services but also of your

overall relationship? If teamwork is a core value, are you capturing feedback on whether people trust each other and understand their roles? Is the performance consistently high across all work groups? Do employee surveys affirm a collaborative environment?

The bottom line is that you can monitor and improve only what you measure. So as you consider your values, think through who must embody them and how you would know if they are being practiced. And if those values are not being lived (whether you are talking about individuals, teams, or organizations), how would that manifest itself negatively?

6. ***Review and update your values and metrics regularly.*** Put a routine in place to assess this on at least a semi-annual or annual basis. Any more frequently is too much change to inflict. An annual review often makes the most sense to correlate your values to your financial plan, your desires for growth, your allocation of capital, and your investment as the marketplace evolves. In that review, make sure that your values still link to your company's purpose as well.

Know that your values will serve as a veritable North Star, especially in difficult times. They'll help you chart the course for your teams, able to sail through any choppy waters—crisis, conflict, scarcity of resources, and more—you might face.

Lead Bigger Through Values

- If your organization and/or team has established values:

    - Do these values ring true to your community and customers?

    - Do they reflect how you operate?

    - Do they reflect your purpose, the corporate culture, and the behavioral norms of your organization?

- Reflect on a time in your career when you felt your personal values linked to your organization's or leader's values. In contrast, how about a time when your values conflicted with your organization and/or your boss?

- In your career, have you or someone you know left a team or organization due to a difference in values?

- How much can you realistically know about your people's professional and—to a degree—personal values? What could you do to gain a better understanding of their values, if needed?

CHAPTER FOUR

PERFORMANCE
DELIVER RESULTS *AND* IMPACT

Your performance matters only if it delivers on your commitments and promises. Connect the work of your team to your stakeholders' priorities. Execute to achieve their desired outcomes. Otherwise, you're simply working for work's sake.

M y experience with a disappointing performance review came in my second assignment as an international process manager at the beginning of my career. I thought I was doing *great,* meeting my objectives and handoffs. But when I met with my boss the day of our annual reviews, I got a rating that was lower than what I thought I'd earned, which meant I didn't get the raise or the bonus I thought I deserved.

Ouch.

I was twenty-something at the time, and at first I was tremendously frustrated.

But as is true with any hard knock, the bigger perspective becomes clear after you've recovered a bit. And this is what I was able to see:

The discrepancy wasn't my boss's fault; it was mine. I had failed to calibrate with him. I wasn't thorough enough; I didn't periodically give him a view into what I was doing. And more than anything else, if I had communicated better, I might have realized sooner that I was too focused on notching outputs, without considering the actual *impact* I was having.

I was laser-focused on my role—negotiating service level contracts with communications providers around the world to ensure the end-to-end quality of our international business products. These agreements made up the customer experience—the handling of disputes, repair response times, and more. They also affected how customers gauged our performance.

My view of success was whether I negotiated the agreement on time, with the current level of quality expected from my company, as was done in the past. In the early months of my job, I was thinking too small. I should have included a wider world of stakeholders, such as our customers, customer support teams, and product teams, who relied on the agreements. Those contracts would have better met their needs if I'd taken the time to speak to them to get their perspectives about the terms I was setting. And in fact, as my boss asked me questions about how our agreements compared to our competitors', I realized that my get-the-task-done mentality was indeed too small. As part of my role, I should have done a rigorous external study of how our competitors were performing and worked that into my strategy of delivering something that was not only tactically complete but also strategically relevant.

Adding these steps would have expanded both my personal influence and my knowledge to create better outcomes for those groups. While there was nothing wrong with the contracts I negotiated, my own expectations for myself prevented me from developing better strategies to include everyone. I did my job and was not reprimanded. But I vividly recall the conversation with my boss on what the better (and bigger) outcome would have been had I focused more inclusively on our partners, our customers, and even our competitors. My boss wasn't accusatory, but his feedback made me realize that I had to think bigger. Without thinking bigger, I'd miss out on opportunities to deliver bigger. It was an *aha!* experience for me. As an ambitious young manager, I remember thinking that this performance review was like getting a C in school. I needed to go for that A!

This was a wake-up call. Leading bigger for yourself means you are almost always also leading bigger for the business at large. There was truth to my boss's assessment that I could have accomplished much more with my efforts.

My task-oriented thinking at this point in my life was linked to my lack of practical experience. Young people coming out of the academic world are used to a formulaic grading system. Your teacher commonly puts it this way: 30 percent of your grade is class participation; 30 percent is quizzes, 10 percent is turning in assignments on time, and so forth. In the business world, this approach goes out the window. The assessment of your performance is subjective, not based strictly on the output you generate. One of the toughest lessons to learn in the transition to the business world is that meritocracy is a myth. Perception is reality and can greatly alter how someone views your performance. When you consider the many different people who are eyeing your performance, it's no wonder that there's no set formula for success. But you can increase your chances of having a positive impact by being strategic and inclusive in your assessment of who matters.

Performance (including how you measure it) means something different to each stakeholder. The bigger leader takes the step to understand and lean toward the performance expectations of those groups. We tend to focus on the performance of any given individual in their role instead of proactively considering the interconnection between roles and across teams. As an example, it's a given that a chief product officer will focus on the number and profitability of new products their team delivers. But the inclusive chief product officer works with Product Development on requirements, timelines, and costs; collaborates with Sales concerning revenue, unit expectations, and pricing; and makes sure that customers' expectations are met and that they're being served well. Inclusion requires that leaders learn what success looks like to each stakeholder and factor that into their work group's metrics, strategy, and plans. They align their team's work to the organizational goals and make sure each team member knows how their objectives connect.

Let's walk through a practical process for measuring performance.

1. Understand Stakeholder Goals

Recall the discussion in chapter 2 about identifying the full scope of your stakeholders. Of course, the end game of work is not just identifying stakeholders. It's delivering what they need, meeting their expectations concerning why you exist, and adding value to them. Whatever the set of stakeholders, each one has a different perspective about what it means for your organization to get the job done. For example:

- Your employees likely prioritize their job security, compensation, career growth, and feeling valued.

- Your managers expect to be equipped with the necessary tools they need to support their people.

- Community advocates may care about your organization's environmental impact and your investments in sustainability.

- Your suppliers will focus on how the amount of business you're winning translates into the work you do together in the marketplace, as defined by customer logos, revenue, or demand.

- Your customers want to reliably receive the products and services they were promised on time and with quality.

One of the most memorable mishaps in my career involved two very visible stakeholders: our customer, the leading nationwide ticket marketplace, and their customer, a famous nineties grunge band. We quickly developed a new toll-free solution that was being used for the first time to launch ticket sales for the band's upcoming concert tour.

Unfortunately, on the go-live date, the service went down because there was an inaccurate understanding of the demand, and the flood of calls exceeded the limits of our capacity. To add insult to injury, there were also miscommunications throughout the attempted delivery process. We were called on the carpet by our customer *and* the band themselves, who chewed us out mercilessly because their fans were distraught and the band's image was suffering. Needless to say, the fact that I myself was a fan of the band brought the importance of understanding our customers' goals to the fore in a big way for me—and this whole experience was a lesson I never forgot.

Though it still looms large in my mind, it's one of many examples of how business can come undone on a global scale when the stakeholders aren't aligned.

During the pandemic, supply chain disruptions exposed the inter-dependence of stakeholders across industries. Companies who considered their supply chains resilient suddenly lacked alternative pathways to source and deliver important components. Manufacturing plants shut down, then couldn't keep up. In the telecom industry, we faced more than just the shortage of cellular devices for consumers and educators alike. There were significant delays in replenishing network communications equipment, which posed challenges we'd never encountered before. As lockdowns shut down manufacturing in China and created unusual shifts in demand, drops and spikes for goods in places like the United States and Europe, shipping was thrown into disarray. Ships were waiting in long queues outside of Los Angeles and Long Beach on the West Coast for a minimum of twelve days before being able to unload goods, creating delays that starved companies of much-needed components and materials while also spiking costs. Ports around the world were having similar experiences, creating higher shipping costs and general chaos. Personnel and crews were not available where they were most needed, and empty containers were in the wrong places.

Companies who could not source key components then found their own production thrown into disarray, and consumers saw prices rise and empty store shelves. As a result of that painful lesson, the dynamic planning of supply chains is now a top priority in most business plans. Worldwide supply chains and shipping, rail, and trucking networks are so complex that big data-style research and software are required to even begin to understand them.

Any manufacturing leader who took a small mindset here, relying on a single supplier, without redundancies, would have felt the most pain. Bigger leaders are often unmasked in times of crisis. Even in the most unprecedented of circumstances, they are able to take a step back, rationally yet urgently assess the situation, then apply a lens that looks beyond just what happened. Their predisposition for inclusion has them considering the ripples caused by the stone skipping across the pond. They consider the ripples affecting their business, their competitors, their customers, their suppliers, and others as they remedy the pain while coming up with more resilient plans for the future.

The intertwined nature of businesses forces you to be thoughtful about the many layers of your work, as well as the layers beyond it. It encourages you not to take for granted anything required for you to perform at your best. By constantly asking yourself where there could be gaps or where a process contains only one main thread of execution, you can plan better and more effectively lead and execute.

2. Set Metrics That Matter

Stakeholders also *measure* your performance differently. Investors and shareholders care more about your financial metrics; industry analysts and your senior leaders may care more about operational ones. Some people will simply warm up to you and your brand because they love your products, your advertisements make them laugh, and what your company does for their community represents a bright spot in their day. To take in the needs of all these various communities requires a multitasking brain; you are receiving signals and prioritizing your next steps accordingly.

I group performance measures into these categories:

- Financial (shareholders, investors, owners)

- Customer (timely delivery, quality product, customer satisfaction, and customer experience (CX))

- Market (an external perspective beyond customers, including the competitive market)

- Operational (internal business processes, supplier relationships, and production)

- People (individuals and teams)

- Organizational/structural (based on specific roles and responsibilities)

Ideally everybody in the organization can connect what they're doing to serving the customer. In my first customer service role, we were responsible for supporting clients from mid- to large-sized companies with communication solutions, which meant we were usually the first people customers reached out to if something wasn't going right. If their calls to us didn't go through, it could mean lost revenues, dissatisfied people, poor levels of service, and more. Our company's product people touted this service, describing it with "99.99 percent reliability." But I learned my customers didn't care about the 99.99 percent after they purchased the service—they expected it to work for them 100 percent of the time. Imagine if the nation's leading flower delivery service went down on Mother's Day—you'd have a lot of stressed-out families and disappointed mothers out there. This was a big moment for both the flower service and their customers, and your delays could have compromised their brand image as well as their trust in your company.

As customer service professionals, we couldn't very well respond to such an issue with "Well, the service is working as advertised." Instead, we quickly created more capacity and rerouted calls. My team strengthened our performance against customer metrics like mean time to repair. But our alternative solutions elevated the company's performance measures, like customer retention and even profit.

In today's world, the importance of understanding customer sentiment has never been higher. Bigger leaders understand that social sentiment, how your brand is being talked about in a variety of online forums, is a reality that can be shaped by experiences and perceptions. This is what it means when your brand truth is on display. Your customers and employees can provide their opinions about your products and services, and even your company culture and behavior. The media, your investors, your future customers, and your potential recruits can all peer into these comments and reviews, so you need to monitor how you are coming across and care about it. There's power in thinking bigger about metrics—even ones that fall outside your direct purview—especially those that reflect where you stand with your customers and your employees. These can provide near-real-time insight that can help you improve. Ignore this at your peril.

3. Contextualize Your Team's Work Vis-à-Vis the Stakeholders' Priorities

Now, if you've gone through the first two steps, you likely have an abundance of stakeholders, needs, and metrics to consider. But no single leader can solely steer all these groups. Though bigger leaders may have responsibility over their own domains, they are still thoughtful about how they influence other parts of the organization to which they're connected.

In large organizations, people may not see the implications of poor performance. I was always amazed at how many individuals don't pay attention to this. No matter the role I've had, I was trained early on to ask these questions of myself and my teams: How does what I do impact the customer, even if it's six degrees of separation away? How does what I do affect the top-line growth and transformation of the company?

Bigger leaders note the connections across performance measures. They seek the bigger picture, not just for themselves but to help others and build "connective tissue" across the organization.

What's difficult is to prioritize what you control as opposed to what you influence. In today's world, you will almost never be able to satisfy all stakeholders equally. There will have to be trade-offs, because your resources—people, time, cash, energy, inventories, and so forth—are finite. Managing risk requires playing an appropriate amount of both offense and defense, and striking that balance between short-term execution and long-term strategy will help you gain clarity on your priorities.

Throughout my career in tech, I've had the good fortune of working with many esteemed, innovative leaders. I'd spend hours with my customers who had dedicated R&D departments, focusing on how our collective ideas and innovation could change the world. I talked to one particular client, who was the head of a famed R&D organization, about the balance between the incubation of ideas and the need to commercialize them.

Before this leader was placed into his role, his organization operated under the belief that invention spawns innovation, and one of the benchmarks of performance was the number of patents they generated. If you were to walk through their hallways, you would see patent certificates proudly displayed in offices, with thermometer-shaped scoreboards tracking the total number of patents each division generated. It was clearly a meaningful performance metric—for them. But what about for the rest of the stakeholders?

Some patents recognize original ideas, but they don't necessarily indicate *impact*. Until the patent becomes applied as an innovation that adds value, its impact is theoretical. Does it address a need? Does it create a new capability that the marketplace will want? If not, the patent will perhaps satisfy only the ego of the person or team who came up with that invention. An investor might say, "Okay, great—but how does that patent translate into new revenue? Or customer growth?" And let's face it: What does the average consumer think about patents? We don't care unless a patent contributes to a product or service that improves our lives, so much so that we're willing to pay for it.

Cautionary Tales: Abandon Values for Performance at Your Peril

What is the worst that can happen when a small leader is put in charge of a large operation? When a leader *doesn't* take the wider perspective or consider the values of the company and the communities it impacts? Let's take the extreme end of small leadership, when a leader takes such a narrow, one-dimensional, often short-term focus on a singular stakeholder or metric—often financial—that other stakeholders are substantially hurt. The driving force behind this can be greed, fraud, ego, or negligence, subverting the company's core values. This is when we see shortsighted decisions, culminating in outcomes such as collapsed industries, prison sentences, environmental disasters, and even death.

Think back on the Deepwater Horizon BP oil spill off the U.S. coast in the Gulf of Mexico. The oil rig explosion, on April 20, 2010, is believed to have killed eleven workers (they were never found). Following that, oil poured into the ocean continuously and catastrophically for months, until it was finally capped four months later. It is considered one of the worst environmental disasters in history, filling the ocean surface to floor with an oil slick the size of Oklahoma, killing marine life, and damaging the coastal economies of multiple states.

The many criminal and civil cases brought against BP and its partners Halliburton and Transocean exposed small leadership on all sides: a rush to complete the well, cost-cutting measures applied to complex drilling processes, and the absence of a culture of safety. The disaster cost over $60 billion in fines to BP, untold dollars in legal fees, public relations damage, damage to the oil industry at large, higher gas prices that affected consumers broadly, and twenty-five thousand jobs lost in the region's commercial and recreational fishing sector.

Leadership had seemingly lost sight of the big picture. Their narrow focus on cost and speed meant they developed a blind spot when it came to safety of their workers and the protection of the ocean environment and coastal communities that were their wider stakeholders. That focus on profit ultimately hurt their bottom line, their investors, and the leadership team's own reputations.

In late 2022, the cryptocurrency exchange FTX collapsed. The U.S. Securities and Exchange Commission charged that CEO Samuel Bankman-Fried had raised more than $1.8 billion from investors under the promise that the platform was run under strict investor protection provisions, while simultaneously misusing funds belonging to FTX's trading customers to cover losses at his privately owned crypto hedge fund Alameda Research. This, regulators commented, was done in service of enriching himself.

On December 13 that year, the new FTX CEO John J. Ray III told a U.S. House committee that in the past, FTX practiced "no bookkeeping." He added, "It was old-fashioned embezzlement."

Bankman-Fried pleaded not guilty but was convicted of all seven counts he faced. Prosecutors made the case that he looted $8 billion from the exchange's users out of greed. It's been called one of the biggest financial frauds in history.

Bankman-Fried was clearly focused on the wrong things, and protection of his own customers' funds fell by the wayside. The alleged criminal and negligent behavior contradicts his professed mission, plastered all over ads taken out in *Vogue* and *The New Yorker*, showing a photo of Bankman-Fried with his arms crossed in front of the text: "I'm in crypto because I want to make the biggest global impact for good."

Ultimately, that failure became the undoing of everyone involved—investors, customers—and deepened the public mistrust of the entire cryptocurrency industry, which sent it into a long "crypto winter." Had

Bankman-Fried been a bigger leader—focusing on the ethics and protection of customer funds—this would never have happened.

Such corporate disasters tend to originate from a focus on profit and a lack of clear purpose and values. Values are stated only for public consumption and contravened in private. Fraud, ego, and negligence are of course about as old as commerce itself, but the stakes are rising as the pace of technology does, too.

For instance, the White House commission report on the BP oil spill found that regulators did not have the authority or knowledge of the complex drilling processes to have noticed the cost-cutting measures that added risk on the Deepwater Horizon. Similarly, FTX was operating in a poorly regulated and poorly understood world of cryptocurrency trading, where both investors and customers were drawn in by FOMO and Bankman-Fried's increasing celebrity, rather than any understanding of the actual technology or business structure.

Now imagine the trouble that can arise if artificial intelligence is developed irresponsibly. The original founders of OpenAI, the makers of ChatGPT, seemed to understand the precarious position of humanity if any of the doomsday scenarios that some envision play out, once the machines become smarter than we are. OpenAI was created as an open-source nonprofit, with a mission "to ensure that artificial general intelligence benefits all of humanity." Later, as researchers worked at OpenAI without sufficient funding for talent and computing power (the computer servers providing the processing power behind ChatGPT 3, for instance, cost $700,000 per day to run), a commercial arm was created as a capped-profit entity, with investor returns capped at one hundred times their investment. Elon Musk, an OpenAI founder who left early on, called it "a closed source, maximum-profit company effectively controlled by Microsoft."

What assurances do we have that leaders at such companies—whether focused on AI or quantum computing or gene editing—will set their gaze wider than their ego or the potential for profit? Especially given that these technological leaps are beyond the capacity for regulators or other watchdogs to keep up with? If the main cohort that has access to decision-making is wealthy geniuses, who have massive fortunes to gain from progress in these high-risk endeavors, should we worry? There is certainly an argument to be made for the inclusion of stakeholders, who can influence the technology that shapes the future and ensure it benefits humanity at large.

The stakes for bigger leadership have never been higher.

Lead Bigger Through Performance

- Revisit your list of stakeholders. What do you do that they care about? What outcomes matter to them? How do they gauge your success?

- Are some stakeholders more important to your work than others? What trade-offs will you have to make? Which metrics do you control and which do you influence?

- Do you have data of your performance trends over time for each group? What feedback systems have you established to understand their priorities?

- How have you evolved your metrics and goals to track short-term and long-term performance?

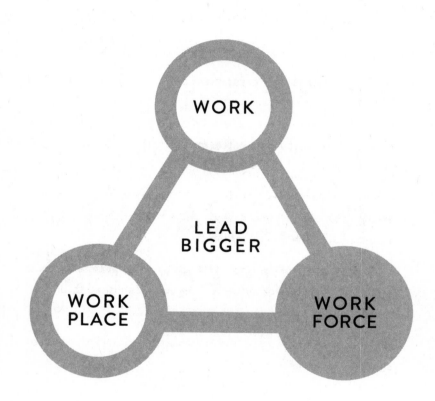

PART TWO

A VITAL, INNOVATIVE WORKFORCE

The **WORKFORCE** represents all the people in any role involved in getting the job done. It often refers to your immediate team, but the workforce in our modern economy is likely composed of people who are not direct employees, such as gig workers, paid influencers, volunteers, and third-party contractors or suppliers. In sum, the workforce simply describes the people required to achieve your desired outcomes.

Let's acknowledge that there is often a chronic tendency to use *corporate speak* when we talk about our people. Corporate speak is jargon consisting of words, acronyms, and phrases typically overused by business professionals. Jargon tends to distance us from people or even turns them into commodities: *human resources* or *human capital,* and phrases like *people are our greatest asset.* When referring to layoffs, we hide behind various euphemisms: *surplus, force management,* and *elimination of redundancies.* When we were referring to cost reductions, before the welcome era of body positivity, a phrase often used was *trimming the fat.* While the use of this is intended to focus people on reducing overhead and improving efficiency, it's clearly problematic. Our words and actions matter, and for bigger leaders, the people *are* the business, and they should guide the way we communicate with them.

Bigger leadership recognizes that workers are—above all else—human. Therefore, we must first start with the **WELL-BEING** of our people. In modern workplaces, this means caring for their health holistically, taking into consideration their physical, mental, emotional, and financial needs. The bigger leader knows that people cannot perform their best if they are not *at* their best. This requires embracing the humanity in each of us, which includes our universal need to belong.

It would be impossible to talk about leading bigger in the workforce without addressing **BIAS,** which I define as a preference or predisposition for, or a prejudice against, something, someone, and more. Biases exist in all of us, both conscious and unconscious, and are continually being shaped as we go through our lives. To illustrate how bias can affect your leadership and your workforce, I've chosen to briefly explore the topic in a special segment on beauty bias, also known as lookism. Interestingly, this is a type of bias that is largely legal and affects every single one of us.

DIMENSIONALITY represents the attributes that make us unique individuals. This chapter seeks to expand our view of how our characteristics and experiences shape who we are, beyond race, gender, and disability. In the beginning stage of my career, I tried to suppress who I was by working to "fit in." It wasn't until I embraced all the facets of my identity—an Asian American woman with an ambivert nature, a people-centric bias, and other elements—that I started to really gain traction as a bigger leader. Because I am a woman of color in the workplace, the fact that I am different has always been obvious. The challenge has been in advancing in an environment that was created by people who were nothing like me.

This section closes with a framework for workforce **VITALITY.** Vitality is the constant renewal of your workforce, as people join your company, grow within it, and eventually leave (but often remain important stakeholders). My framework for vitality consists of eight stages. Too often, managers tend to lead small by focusing only on the job at hand, heavily prioritizing performance management. Your workforce is forever changing because of the dynamics of the labor market, the inevitable fact that workers grow older, the evolution of skill sets, the nature of the jobs to be done, and the impact of new technologies. Vitality means you are tending to the health of your organization through nurturing your people at every stage. I'll share leadership suggestions, practices, and policies to help you lead bigger so your workforce can contribute the most today and transform themselves for tomorrow.

CHAPTER FIVE

WELL-BEING

ELEVATE PERFORMANCE
THROUGH CARE AND BELONGING

For people to perform at their best, they must be at their best. Amid a global mental health crisis, most people say work is a source of at least one mental health challenge. Leaders aren't therapists, but they can drastically improve their team's outcomes by focusing on employee well-being and fostering a culture of belonging.

As I approached my fifties, I could feel how the decades-long grind of my career and the demands of raising a family had taken a toll. One of the pressures included a career-driven decision to move to Texas, triggered by a once-in-a-lifetime opportunity to work directly for a legendary industry leader whose inspirational origin story—at age ten he emigrated by himself from Cuba to the United States; only he was allowed on the plane when his family all attempted to board—set the foundation for his role as one of the biggest leaders in our company. My daughters were in vital stages of their development, one a rising eighth grader and the other a rising high school junior, and my husband was their primary caregiver. In Texas, we would have no family or friends nearby. All of this meant that the social and emotional pressures for my family were off the charts. My own health had taken a back seat at best. I was stressed both at work and at home. My exercise regimen had been replaced by the grind of travel, and I didn't have friends and family around me for constant grounding as I did back in my home state of New Jersey. Meanwhile, some of my friends approaching their milestone birthdays were in the best condition of their lives, and I was in the exact opposite place. I knew I needed to make a change.

Being the ever-budget-conscious daughter of immigrants, I've always been a coupon clipper. So of course I used Groupon to discover what was out there, eventually finding my way to fitness boxing at a new TITLE Boxing Club. On impulse I signed up for a full-year membership at their grand opening, figuring that the financial commitment of over a hundred bucks a month would increase my accountability.

For the first couple of months, I couldn't even make it through a one-hour class. But I quickly fell in love with the challenge. Boxing requires such physical, mental, and emotional focus that you can't be distracted in any way. Its rigorous interval training pushed me beyond my perceived limits. It's also an incredible stress reliever, given the license to punch at will.

I've often told my colleagues to make sure they don't wait until a midlife milestone (or crisis) to have that epiphany. We now know that physical health and emotional resilience are the building blocks to feeling strong and showing up in the world as your best self. This is foundational for being your best at work, too.

But the reality is that by and large, most workers cannot access solutions to their mental health challenges, which may include more severe forms of depression and anxiety. Society at large is undergoing a mental health crisis. The U.S. surgeon general reports that a staggering 76 percent of workers struggle with at least one symptom of a mental health condition, and McKinsey research found that these employees are "four times more likely to want to leave their organization. They are also more likely to report low job satisfaction, engagement, or other signifiers of positive workplaces."

The pressures in the workforce are real: Many feel stress, burnout, exhaustion, loneliness, depression, and anxiety, to the point where these mental health behavioral disorders are the leading cause of disability. A third of workers felt depressed or anxious at least once a week. These were emotions that most people would not be comfortable revealing, especially at work. There is a bias that these feelings are signs of weakness, as opposed to simply part of being human.

Contrary to common perception, mental health struggles are not relegated to one generation or segment of the population; every demographic is hurting. The findings from McKinsey's global survey across fifteen countries and nearly fifteen thousand employees tell us what we should already know, but which bears mentioning given the stigmas associated with mental health struggles: "No demographic appears immune to mental-health challenges. Our survey reveals that employees face mental-health challenges irrespective of their country, industry, age group, role, or gender." Most leaders are, of course, not mental health professionals, and they must respect the boundaries around these sensitive issues. Yet the responsibility to safeguard the well-being of the workforce has landed at their feet, due to the expectations of their people and the link between well-being and performance results, and frankly, because 84 percent of workers say their workplace has contributed to at least one mental health challenge. Well-being is now a leadership responsibility.

Linking Well-Being and Inclusion

Like people, mental health is also diverse, and it shows up in different ways across different demographics. Let's look at how a few particular dimensions vary in their mental health struggles.

The generations are experiencing stark differences in the state of their well-being. According to SHRM, "Millennials, who make up the largest segment of the workforce, are the loneliest generation. Three in ten Millennials always or often feel lonely. . . . At work, 66 percent of Millennials found it hard to make friends, compared to less than 23 percent of Baby Boomers." Gen Z has higher rates of anxiety and depression than any other generation at work. Gen X is shouldering intense caregiving responsibilities, and financial worries hurt Gen Xers' mental health the most out of all the generations. Clearly a single approach would not be equally effective across the generations.

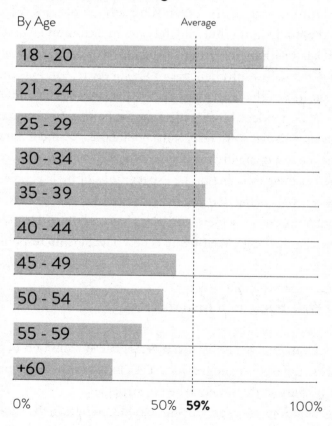

Share of respondents reporting at least one mental-health challenge

By Age   Average

Age	
18 - 20	
21 - 24	
25 - 29	
30 - 34	
35 - 39	
40 - 44	
45 - 49	
50 - 54	
55 - 59	
+60	

0%   50% **59%**   100%

Source: "Present company included: Prioritizing mental health and well-being for all," October 2022, McKinsey Health Institute, www.mckinsey.com. Copyright © 2024 McKinsey & Company. All rights reserved. Data from McKinsey and Company exhibit adapted with permission.

And just as one size does not fit all across the generations, wellness and mental health needs vary across roles and industries. I have spent over half of my corporate career in front of customers across sales and service roles. We were on call all the time—if the customer needed us, we were there. From the days of pagers to always-on mobile connectivity, it was virtually impossible to untether ourselves from the job. Some people thrive in jobs like this. Others who need better balance might do well to avoid them at all costs.

Recall the intense pressures on front-line employees during the lockdowns, when grocery store workers, healthcare providers, and many others became essential workers overnight. Our frontline workers at AT&T, those who were out in the field taking care of the network and our customers, and employees in our retail stores faced the same pressures. Particularly in the early months, stress was off the charts for many of our people. To better support them, we provided enhanced programs and resources focused on taking care of their mental health. Bigger leaders continuously reframe their roles in the context of the moment, trying to address the unique needs of people at any given point in time. The pandemic was of course dramatic, but situations and conditions constantly change. Bigger leaders strive to anticipate and stay on top of changes in the economy and society so that they can effectively address the needs of their people as those changes unfold.

Consider how teachers and educators now face new challenges as topics such as gender identity, race, politics, and religion-based ideologies have permeated the classroom, topics often brought up by the students themselves. Then we see complexity arise from the reactions of parents and school boards, even third parties, all of whom have varying agendas. Teachers and educators are under incredible amounts of stress. The opportunity to lead bigger, especially the importance of prioritizing well-being, exists beyond corporations and is relevant in every context.

Another factor is gender. Women in the workforce are under additional strain due to childbirth, child- and eldercare, and physiological reasons, a topic we'll explore further in chapter 10. Team members who identify as transgender or nonbinary face mental health challenges in the workplace related to their fear of discrimination and harassment. People who live in rural communities often have less access to mental health treatment, from providers with less expertise. This is not solely a U.S. phenomenon but a global one, too. Country-specific cultural nuances come into play when we consider the discussion and treatment of these mental health challenges.

Share of respondents reporting at least one mental-health challenge

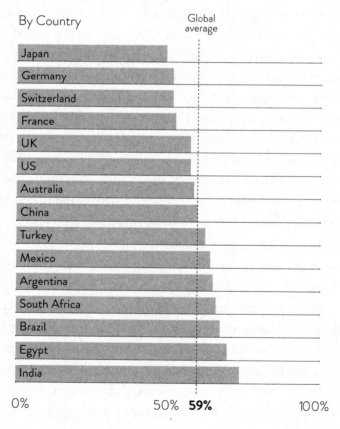

Source: "Present company included: Prioritizing mental health and well-being for all," October 2022, McKinsey Health Institute, www.mckinsey.com. Copyright © 2024 McKinsey & Company. All rights reserved. Data from McKinsey and Company exhibit adapted with permission.

For example, in Japan, unlike in many countries, mental health treatment is affordable and widely available, thanks to national health insurance. But almost 70 percent of people want to handle their mental health struggles on their own.

The stigma associated with mental health issues varies in different communities and environments. While 30 percent of the U.S. workforce would not turn to any workplace resource if they needed mental health assistance, the Asian American and Pacific Islander (AAPI) and Black communities are the most reluctant to access these resources due to concerns around privacy and stigma. American Indian and Alaskan natives are two times more likely to be uninsured and have the highest prevalence of chronic health conditions. The LGBTQ+ community is two and a half times more likely to be diagnosed with anxiety, depression, and substance misuse. As you reflect on these stats, remember that we are all more than just one thing, including our struggles.

Your employees have their own individual experiences with medical professionals, services, and healthcare systems. Bigger leaders should help make these resources as available and accessible as possible. This means creating an action plan for supporting people directly and inclusively. Here are some thoughts on how to do that:

Have multiple touchpoints with your employees. Connection is a lifeline. Both scheduled and ad hoc check-ins can address feelings of isolation, rich soil for many mental health challenges. Encourage those who may be isolated by introducing them into work cohorts, like employee groups, volunteer community activities, and mentoring circles, to develop camaraderie. Leading with empathy doesn't need to be done with lots of overhead; in fact, a practice I adopted early on in my career was to send handwritten birthday and service anniversary notes. My long-standing obsession with Post-it Notes (which has since been passed on to my daughters) was helpful in my leadership roles as I constantly sought impromptu opportunities to share thoughts, provide comments, say hello, and simply connect with my people in a more authentic, informal way.

Encourage connections outside of work. Side hustles have traditionally been viewed negatively, but not everybody can fully thrive in their life just through their day job. That doesn't make them or their roles unworthy. As leaders, we need to acknowledge that some people need other engagements in their lives, and as long as these don't constitute a conflict of interest or negatively impact their performance on the job, we should cheer them on.

Monitor how your teams are doing. Don't underestimate the effect of national or world events on your people. Take a regular pulse of the well-being of your teams, but don't stay wedded to a scheduled process. Annual reviews are often insufficient, given how fast the environment and the marketplace change. Establish consistent surveys gauging trust, transparency, and connection.

Normalize mental health. Leaders need to learn how to be vulnerable themselves and appropriately share their own struggles. In the early days of the pandemic, when I was the CEO of AT&T Business, the fact that I was working around the clock limited how I expressed the pressures I felt, even with my closest loved ones. The weight of my responsibilities—for my customers, my employees, the business as a whole, and my loved ones—felt unbearable at times. And for the first ninety days, I thought that I would break. During this time, I felt like I was not fulfilling any of my roles well—as leader, team member, mom, wife, daughter, sister, or friend. I had a litany of fears: I might not ever see my parents again; my loved ones were going to get sick; the people important to me were going to die; I was going to get infected. To normalize these feelings, I decided to write about what was going through my mind, sharing my fears via internal email and LinkedIn. I wanted to let people know that it was more than okay to be vulnerable. I gave my team the license to open up and reach out to one another. Embracing our vulnerability and our humanity helped us deepen our connection to one another and made us stronger, as individuals and as a team.

Celebrate the humanness of your organization. This is best done through storytelling. Highlight the incredible things your people do in the community, at work, or within their families. With their permission, talk about the resources they accessed, boosting others' awareness of these benefits. Our employees often don't know the various leaves, programs, and resources available to them. And discussing how you work flexibly or what you did with your paid time off or on your vacation reinforces the idea that it's okay for other people to do the same. Like one of my former colleagues would say: go on vacation, stay on vacation…*be* vacation.

Offer help with managing workloads. One of the most important things bigger leaders can do is recognize that work does play a role in people's stress, burnout, and exhaustion. Leaders can reach out to individuals with the intention of alleviating their workload: *Wow, I see you're doing a lot. Can I offer some help to assist you in prioritizing? You don't need to attend that meeting. Why don't we give this assignment to a junior colleague to help them grow and take some stress off your plate? Why don't you take some time off?* Proactively offering solutions—without judgment—sets the precedent that it's okay to admit you need help with completing a task or that you need time off to de-stress.

Factor in financial well-being. We're talking a lot about mental health and emotional health and its relationship with physical health. But the importance of financial well-being is especially timely because, as leaders and managers, we typically have no idea how this is playing out in employees' lives. We're aware of our employees' wages and benefits, but we don't know what they need to survive and what survival means for them. An employee may have an obligation to care for their parents or fund college for their nieces and nephews. They may have escaped from an abusive marriage with their credit destroyed. They may be in a decades-long financial recovery from a natural disaster or health crisis or have massive loans to pay off. In some cases, financial challenges can undo an employee's health and focus.

When building benefits packages or company policy, bigger leaders ensure that their employees are financially supported by offering financial wellness training (including seminars on key topics such as taxes, debt management, cash flow, and savings) while also making available financial consultants for one-on-one support, making sure that the benefits measure up to market (retirement plans, health saving accounts) each year, and more. It should be a given that employers provide a living wage for their employees, no matter their role or geographical location.

Overall, help the people on your team optimize their own life equations. This may sound counterintuitive, coming from a driven CEO type, but all of us have only one life to live. Yes, your work is part of that life, but it is not your whole life. Your job is what you do, but it is *not* who you are. And now more than ever, people are waking up to this reality and want to prioritize their well-being.

Creating Belonging for Each Member of Your Workforce

Today, we desire to work in an environment where we feel like we belong, but on our terms rather than someone else's.

In my early corporate career, women had to dress in ways that mimicked male business dress codes. (Confession: I had a fashion allergy to pearls and cotton bow blouses, no matter how much I tried to embrace the outfits that would help me "fit in.") Women were coached never to talk at work about having kids at home, lest their colleagues remember they were mothers, which somehow implied a risk to their commitment to the job! (Ever wonder why we specify "working moms," but never "working dads"?)

When I started my career, I felt like an anomaly. I was young, female, and Asian in a field then dominated by older white men. I felt pressure from myself and my counterparts to fit into a corporate archetype I wasn't conventionally a part of. It started with the scratchy cotton blouses, which seemed to be the uniform of choice for corporate women. Both the discomfort and lack of individual expression in the attire rubbed me the wrong way (figuratively and literally!). But I conformed for several years because other young women in my situation were also dressing that way and I thought it was what I had to do to get ahead. I also felt challenged by how I wanted to communicate and present myself. I intentionally developed a manner of speaking that was both direct and warm so I could better connect with people. Because it was obvious that I was different—in age, tenure, gender, race, education, and more—I was mindful of how I demonstrated my authenticity. Early on, the diversity of my ideas and my problem-solving were the indicators of my authenticity. It was only later in my career that I allowed my authenticity to show up even more—in how I built relationships, the words I chose to communicate with, the style I'd use depending on my audience and objectives. During those early days, I was both mindful and purposeful in how I chose to show up because it was obvious that I was different.

I was reminded of these differences in my very first role at AT&T. My boss told me she wanted to put me in charge while she went on a month-long vacation, which was already scheduled for six months after my start date. We worked on getting me ready, and on the first day she was gone, my colleagues transformed her office, labeling anything that was hers as mine. Rather than feeling embarrassed or indignant, I actually thought it was hilarious. To some it may have seemed a light form of hazing, but to me, it was their way of acknowledging and including me in the group, albeit temporarily as their supervisor.

Unfortunately, not all of my early interactions were so constructive. There were plenty of times when my contributions were brushed off with "Kiddo, you just don't have the experience on this one." Or when my ideas were mansplained over and over, no matter how assertive I was. It was difficult to be the only female voice in the room, let alone the only woman of color in the entire department!

There was an expectation by some that I should just put my head down and work hard—after all, aren't all Asians good at that? When I first broached my interest in advancing my career to a supervisor, he was surprised and said that he "wouldn't have expected me" to want that. I'm still not sure what was the source of his bias—perhaps it was my lack of experience or exposure, or simply the fact that I didn't match the profile of what he thought an aspiring leader should be like.

It was during these first five years of my career when I also ran into the fairly universal assumption that as a single person, I should carry more of the weight of work, especially when it came to after-hours and the weekends. I found this irritating, often musing to myself why people thought that the notion of "family first" applied only to certain views of family. Silently, I vowed to think and lead bigger if given the opportunity. I'd ensure that there wasn't an inadvertent bias toward people who weren't married or who weren't parents in the most traditional sense. Bottom line, bigger leaders know better. And they work hard to apply expectations fairly and inclusively. As I said earlier, interpersonal flexibility is key.

Small leadership forces everyone into the same box—or square cubicle. Leading bigger creates team environments where people can be their true selves and still belong.

Back when I considered myself an introverted engineer, I endured many unbearable happy hours, mostly because I was told that it was important to be seen. In fact, one of my bosses said that I needed to show up at these if I ever hoped to get close to the powerful, popular crowd. My level of discomfort measured 11 on a scale of 10, partially because I was always the only woman of color and oftentimes the youngest person in the room. I also wasn't a big drinker. I finally worked for a leader who provided me with a slick way to handle these events. Show up fifteen minutes late and get a tonic water or a ginger ale, some beverage that looks adult (to circumvent the "Can I get you a drink? Why aren't you drinking?" commentary). Intentionally circle the room twice and then go. Done in no more than an hour. As time went on, I also learned that if you brought a buddy, these experiences were much more tolerable and even occasionally enjoyable.

Belonging is central to all humans, as Julia Taylor Kennedy and Pooja Jain-Link of the think tank Coqual write: "Psychologists rank our need to belong on par with our need for love." We come into this world as part of something greater than ourselves. Think about the language used in various cultures—villages, tribes, clans, dynasties—or your home bases in school—homeroom, class, teams, societies, clubs. Then there are your affiliations as an adult: your alma mater, major, hometown, place of worship, neighborhood, or profession. These are logical groupings of commonality that foster that sense of belonging.

Inclusion is an action; belonging is the essential outcome of that action.

When inclusion becomes systemic, belonging is what results. And belonging can be manifested in meaningful sustained connection, community, comfort, and deep engagement. While a sense of belonging is familiar to all of us, we haven't always addressed belonging in professional work cultures. So let's place this in the context of leading bigger in the workforce.

Humans have always had to work. Certainly we do work to *survive,* to provide for both ourselves and our loved ones. What each of us needs to survive, though, is quite personal and spans a diverse range of requirements such as a base level income for shelter and sustenance, as well as access to healthcare. But our work is also what we do to *thrive.* We want to be fulfilled. We want to find meaning and grow. We want to become more than who we currently are. We want to feel trusted, valued, and appreciated. We want to solve problems and be recognized for our contributions, and many of us seek passion in our work, in pursuit of our greater calling.

Perhaps surprisingly, 34 percent of people feel a greater sense of belonging at work than in their neighborhood or place of worship. But not everyone strives to find deep meaning in their work. They need to belong in another context, fulfilling some aspiration, passion project, or ideal. In these instances, the day job may simply be necessary to provide a path for that person's bigger purpose, which can turn into a meaningful side hustle.

A lack of belonging can also lead people to suffer from the so-called impostor syndrome, the belief that one is inadequate and not qualified, at risk of being seen as a fraud. This struggle is commonly shared among high achievers. Bigger leaders learn how to move from self-doubt and the fear of not meeting goals to an ongoing quest for excellence and realization of their fullest potential.

In 2019, I had the opportunity to host clients and colleagues at the Super Bowl. The Saturday night before the game, the Foo Fighters were playing. I am a *huge* Foo Fighters fan (and no, they weren't the band that chewed us out earlier in this book!), so this was one of those magical moments where my personal and professional passions collided in a way that couldn't have made me happier. I was rocking it out, singing every word. I even got a selfie with Dave Grohl!

Because I was such an obvious fangirl, I built a personal rapport with clients and partners who shared my love of the Foo Fighters—in ways we never would have otherwise bonded. At one point I did spot an executive who was definitely not a fan. He was sitting on a sofa by himself—earplugs firmly in place—looking as enthusiastic as if he were waiting for a bus. In his company at large, he was an ambitious king of the corporate mountain. At this concert, he was a disengaged king of the couch. I found it so interesting that I felt that I belonged in that environment, whereas he clearly did not. Belonging is both situational and conditional, ultimately determined by how we each feel. To his credit, he didn't leave the concert too early and professionally engaged with the group on his way out.

Of course, we wouldn't want to be too hard on someone who isn't into loud music, barely enduring a rock concert, just as I hoped that my quick loops at happy hours were not the source of ridicule. While common interests are generally a good thing, the bigger leader must be mindful that these gatherings do not inadvertently create isolated work groups. (If the Foo Fighters Fan Club becomes an impenetrable work clique, a bigger leader should intervene!)

When work cliques do form, it's usually not deliberate or for bad reasons, and the bigger leader doesn't assume it is. Oftentimes this is the way it is because that's how it's always been. People may have bonded over a sport like golf, or they traveled together and had some shared experiences. Maybe it's a shared passion for fancy cars or a similar sense of humor. It takes just one person to bring positive change and mix things up a bit. You can be the bigger leader and engage while also helping others to experience the richness of new perspectives. One of my favorite career memories involves hunting. When our headquarters was moved to Texas, we found an expanded selection of potential team-building activities, including hunting. I was told that women typically did not participate in this. After accepting this limitation for several years, a (female) colleague of mine and I decided that we would give it a try, joining a group of our male peers on a mixed bag hunt. I had no training when the event came around the next year. Suffice it to say that our peers were both surprised and welcoming. Lots of laughter was had (with me and about me). In fact, I had a bout of beginner's luck and was given the temporary nickname "Annie Oakley." Sometimes the way to reconfigure these inner circles is just to do it. Make the bigger effort.

If this sounds like a lot of work, that's because it is. Belonging is often viewed as touchy-feely, a soft skill, but it is actually tied directly to performance. In that vein, I see it as a kind of God particle in your company culture. Engineer nerd moment: *God particle* is the colloquial name for the Higgs boson—discovered in the study of particle physics. The Higgs boson, in the simplest terms, creates a field that enables other fundamental matter in the universe to have mass. It gives shape and size to everything that exists. In many ways this is a perfect analogue for how belonging can similarly provide shape and meaning to your company culture. Belonging activates every individual on the team, giving them strength and the opportunity to shine in the face of change.

Let's look at a set of experiments done by coaching platform BetterUp, in which they evaluated the task performance of individuals included or excluded in a virtual ball-toss game. The game assigned three people to play, but unbeknownst to the participant, two of the players were bots programmed to behave in a way that was inclusive (throwing the ball equally between the players) or in a manner that would exclude the participant (throwing the ball to the participant only 3 percent of the time). Then the participant was intermittently given the ability to win cash prizes by doing some simple math problems. And here was the crux of the experiment: Sometimes they were told that the cash earned would go only to them, and other times that it would be shared among the three team members. Given that the participant would also benefit from the shared prizes in the form of a one-third payout, this was designed to test the degree to which the participant would behave in service of the collective benefit, including their own, despite their inclusion or exclusion. When included in the ball-toss segment, participants worked as hard on tasks for cash payouts for the whole team as they would on tasks where they were paid only for their own individual benefit. When participants were excluded, their performance remained high when they would get all the cash from the tasks, but their efforts on tasks that would pay the team saw an immediate 25 percent decline, even though this would hurt the test subject's own financial gain from the shared prize. And once an individual was excluded, that person's persistence and performance would drop on future tasks as well. And this was after what was meant to be a two-minute-long "fun" team project!

It's not a leap to imagine how this could play out in real life, where an excluded team member might also feel less inclined to go above and beyond to benefit a team that is not fully accepting them as a member.

Does belonging still feel too abstract for you to focus on? Research has demonstrated that fostering belonging leads to a *56 percent increase in performance,* as well as a cascade of better outcomes like reduced sick days, less turnover, and drastically higher employer net promoter scores. A net promoter score measures the willingness of someone to recommend—a company, a product, a service—to a friend, family members, or colleagues.

If you're convinced that belonging matters, you'll want to scan your organization to find parts of the workforce that might feel left out. The American Psychological Association has found that certain segments are particularly likely to feel lower levels of belonging:

- Individual contributors, middle management, and frontline workers

- Black and Hispanic workers

- Younger workers, as compared with workers who are age forty-four and older

The "belonging scores" in the following chart are probably not absolute, but they do represent a snapshot in time when the research was conducted (Coqual, 2020). This data forces us to question how parts of our workforce experience belonging differently. What groups have different levels of belonging? Perhaps people who aren't in sales? People who didn't grow up in the city where your headquarters is located? Maybe those without a graduate degree?

Coqual's The Power of Belonging:
Professionals' Median Belonging Scores

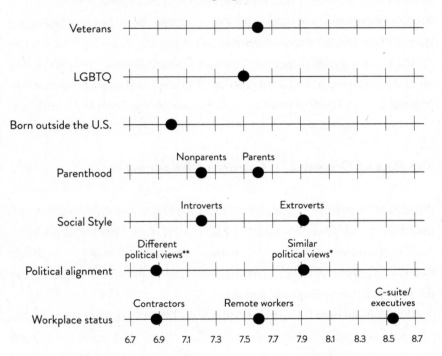

*Professionals who share political views with most of their colleagues
** Professionals who do not share political views with most of their colleagues
Source: Center for Talent Innovation, (Coqual, 2020)
Coqual, The Power of Belonging: What it is and Why it Matters in Today's Workplace, 2020.

Once you look across your teams and discover who might feel less belonging, you have found new pockets of energy that can be unleashed. Bring those folks in from the edges, and you will unlock new sources of strength for your organization.

What you do to support belonging will differ by person and group, but these efforts are not intended to exclude anyone. You certainly don't want to put initiatives in place that then make those who feel a high sense of belonging suddenly feel excluded. Even as you seek to engage those who feel like they are on the fringes, you can enlist the help of those in the center—often in the majority and at the top of the hierarchy. For example, later in this chapter we discuss how supervisors were teamed up with women of color to elevate understanding and belonging.

The key point is that belonging is for *everyone*. Belonging is a key ingredient for culture, and your culture is your biggest competitive advantage. Consider that given sufficient time and resources, your competitor can replicate what you do and what you have. But the one thing they cannot replicate is the set of people you have and the culture you collectively embrace.

The Role of Dissent in a Culture of Belonging

An inclusive culture of belonging welcomes dissonance, disagreement, and differences. One easy tactic I've leveraged since I became a manager back in the nineties is the use of an anonymous digital mailbox so people could share their feedback anytime. I wanted to provide a risk-free way for people to share their thoughts.

As the pandemic hit and our familiar daily routines were severely disrupted, I sent out weekly notes to my global team that consisted of both timely business updates and personal reflections. When U.S. Supreme Court Justice Ruth Bader Ginsburg passed away in 2020, I paid homage to her in my weekly note; I felt a special connection with her given our shared alma mater, Cornell University. I received about half a dozen anonymous emails, presumably from my employees, saying that I should keep my liberal views to myself (along with some additional choice phrases and words). To be clear, in my note, I had made no statement in support of her rulings or concerning my own political views. My intent was to recognize a transformative person in our history, a life well lived, and a fellow Cornellian. Instead of debating their comments, I gave agency to these anonymous voices, too. After all, I had established an open-door policy and encouraged anyone to reach out to me through an anonymous mailbox if they were uncomfortable contacting me directly. To encourage continued dialogue I acknowledged their feedback in my next town hall. While wrapping up the session, I thanked those who had taken the time to provide feedback and said that I wanted to talk about some specific comments I had received. I read the concerns out loud and apologized to those who felt that I had crossed some line, as that wasn't my intention. I shared my rationale and reinforced the fact that I was not intending to make a political statement in any way. I closed the dialogue by reinforcing our commitment to inclusion, emphasizing the importance of openness to all perspectives. Enabling and encouraging constructive feedback is key.

However, you must draw the line if the commentary becomes derogatory, discriminatory, or unprofessional—reinforcing the basic leadership expectation to respect one another and embody our collective values.

One thing to watch out for here: Values and ideology are different. In the workplace, values and mutual respect have a place, but ideology is personal. More on that later.

Surrounding ourselves with diverse points of view typically brings some level of dissonance. In this dissonance comes the chance to learn and grow. When someone doesn't agree with me, I purposefully make sure they have time to speak their mind; foundationally, the bigger leader pushes people to have a seat and a voice at the table, coupled with the opportunity to use their influence. There is a method in the madness that ensues when you allow a team to express a wide range of views: You get better decisions, feedback, and connections. This is why I always included my key partners around the table—from legal to finance to human resources to public relations to corporate strategy—in any major launch. It was to ensure a balanced set of voices who would not simply align against our business unit objectives, but rather push us, and especially me as the leader of the team, to ensure we had thought through the trade-offs, risks, and priorities.

Of course, collaboration is different from consensus. Collaboration is working with others to create or produce something. Consensus, on the other hand, is agreement reached by the group as a whole. With difficult issues and decisions, consensus is often impossible, nor should it be the primary objective. One of my indicators of success was to gauge the timing and degree of consensus on a complex project. If there was consensus too early in the process, I saw this as a red flag indicating that perhaps I hadn't brought together a diverse enough set of people and/or that I hadn't yet established an environment that made it safe for people to speak up. As a team, you want to get to the best decisions—this requires diverse perspectives to elevate the discussion. Getting everyone to agree on what path should be followed is unlikely—which is the fallacy of consensus. But getting everyone to understand the *why* behind the chosen path, while building alignment, is the power of collaboration.

Bigger leaders don't shy away from debate or discussion of new ideas or even from failure. They encourage these while seeking to understand the viewpoints of others and engage differently. It's a continuous journey of honing your practice of inclusive leadership. When I expanded my learning about gender identity, thanks to the inclusive awareness raised largely by my Gen Z network (which includes my daughters), I realized the phrases I was used to—for example, *ladies and gentlemen* and *all men and women*—needed to be modified. These could now be considered incomplete, divisive, or not inclusive, especially when addressing as many as thirty-five thousand people in the organization. Certainly my intention in using these words was never to offend or exclude, but rather to include. What was appropriate yesterday may not be appropriate today—whether it be words, behaviors, processes, policies, or systems. That's how progress works. So now I simply say, "ladies, gentlemen, and all people" and "all men, women, and team members." I didn't give up my language, I just enhanced it to be bigger—which was the whole purpose of my using the words anyway. Certainly, there are ideologies that arise in these considerations, but remember we concentrate on values in the workplace. The value here was to create a sense of belonging and respect for everyone. To me, this was a growth opportunity because I want to intentionally relate to all people, and this language has helped me do so.

Gender identity and inclusivity are sensitive topics in many circles. We are aware of nuances that were not previously considered, particularly the idea that one's gender identity exists apart from one's biological sex at birth. Unfamiliar ideas and change can create fear and reaction, sometimes overreaction. Personal ideologies become a barometer, rather than shared values, and there is suddenly a fray of controversy. Facing this, many company leaders will seek to achieve a basic tolerance of different views. I contend that for high-performing teams, even that isn't enough.

Tolerating is something you do when you have a pebble in your shoe. Working on a team where you are barely tolerated is not going to bring the best out of anyone. In order for teams to interact with high

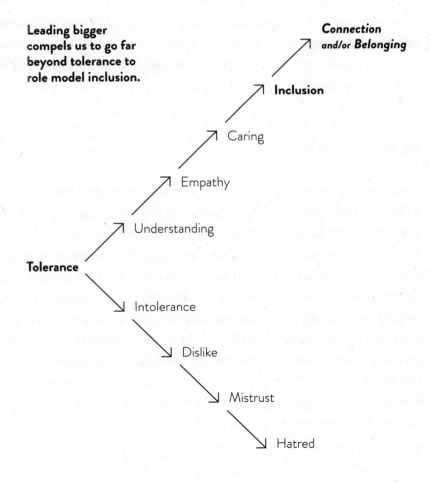

Leading bigger compels us to go far beyond tolerance to role model inclusion.

Connection and/or **Belonging**

Inclusion

Caring

Empathy

Understanding

Tolerance

Intolerance

Dislike

Mistrust

Hatred

trust, we need to move beyond tolerance to understanding, empathy, and caring. And ultimately the objective is inclusion, which results in meaningful connection and/or belonging. We must bring that both to marginalized and underrepresented people *and* to those who are uncomfortable with or even fear change as well.

It might be hard to imagine moving everyone at a large and diverse organization all the way from basic tolerance to true belonging. But think about the risks if you don't. For one, some folks on your team will be operating like the excluded participant in the ball-toss research experiment. And inevitably, if we don't move forward, we backslide. Sadly, what lies on the other side of tolerance can too readily be hatred. We've seen this show up through racism, sexism, ageism, transphobia, xenophobia, and more. And the reality is that this hatred manifests itself in words, behaviors, and actions—even violence. Clearly this has no place within the modern workforce nor in a culture of belonging.

Tactics and Practices

Here's the good news. Workers often report that the most important factor in belonging is cost-effective and easy to implement: the simple check-in. Asking your employees how they're doing, both personally and profession-ally, is a more effective way to create belonging than public recognition, being invited to executive meetings or out-of-office events, or being copied on communications with senior leaders, according to EY's research. I found that the most effective ways of checking in were informal and impromptu. You don't want to add the burden of yet another meeting or have your people wondering about the purpose of the check-in that pops up on their calendar. I prefer to "randomly" text or IM someone—even dropping them a voice mail from time to time. This way they know that I'm thinking about them and that I'm here to help.

Let's review other practices to develop belonging:

Be intentional with the spotlight. In industries like tech, where only 5 percent of the employees are women of color, discussions at conferences become known not as panels, but as "man-nels," because they so consistently exclusively feature white men. Think about whom you choose to celebrate and select to be speakers at your sessions. People want to feel seen and heard, and the old adages that "representation matters" and "you can't be what you can't see" still ring true for many.

Create groups that organize a nucleus of people. As initially designed, conventional DEI practices were isolated in nature. You focused on your Black employees, women employees, Hispanic employees, LGBTQ+ employees, parents, and so forth. Oftentimes these lacked the structural support bringing those different dimensions of identity together to set meaningful change. And in many ways, these new "inner circles" could create a sense that those outside the circle were excluded.

Too often DEI practices focus heavily on representation and the specific development of individuals from the group. While these can be helpful steps, if that's all you're doing, real progress won't be made because nothing has been done to address the systemic issues, the policies, practices, and cultural biases that continue to serve as barriers. Too often, companies use these tactics to mitigate criticism by displaying these meager bread crumbs as if they represent a golden path toward actual inclusion.

These conventional DEI practices also undermine women of color. One in five Americans is a woman of color today, and they will represent the majority of women in the United States by the year 2060. Importantly, women of color have significant leadership ambitions: 41 percent of women of color want to be top executives, compared with 27 percent of white women.

The lack of a dedicated focus on women of color became apparent to me in the last decade of my corporate career at AT&T. I saw strong progress in the development and advancement of women, with several high-impact programs in support of them, many of which I was part of. However, there wasn't any particular focus on women of color. What resulted was steady gains in the careers of white women, while the proportion of women of color who succeeded was far less. These talented women were being disproportionately left behind. Meanwhile, I was actively engaged in employee resource groups and networks and witnessed the growing connection between Black, Latina, and Asian women—within their own silos. My concerns were backed up by data gathered by McKinsey and Lean In in their third annual Women in the Workplace study in 2017, which found that if companies employ a one-size-fits-all approach for all women, the gap for women of color actually widens. I wanted to do something about it.

I partnered with our chief diversity officer and two fellow women of color executives who served as my co-champions to assemble cohorts of women of color who had participated in our existing programs for women. We asked for their input on these programs, which led to heartfelt candid dialogues that guided us in the creation of an initiative focusing on the connections between women of color. Hundreds of women and their supervisors went through the multi-month experience, which included learning experiences facilitated by outside experts, peer-to-peer sessions not only with one another but with other women of color leaders at different companies, and workshops with their supervisors to share candid learnings and insights. At completion, we hosted a "graduation" and heard countless testimonials concerning how the experience had changed the women's lives for the better. Of note, the women themselves felt more confident in their identities, including the supervisors who helped them become aware of their talent and the obstacles they faced. Many women in the program noted how much they appreciated that this wasn't another program meant to "fix" them, but rather an attempt to clear away the systemic obstacles in their way and to embrace them in belonging.

My takeaway: Inclusion should not be a zero-sum game. It needs to bring along those who have power, compelling them to extend their influence and circle of belonging to those on the fringes. Really, that's what we are missing in the current DEI conversations. Growing the pie for any one group does not take slices away from others. That kind of thinking comes from a scarcity mindset. *If you win, I lose.* Have you ever felt the tension when free pizza is brought into work and there's not quite enough for everyone? It's a terrible feeling, you and your hungry colleagues awkwardly jockeying for that last slice of pepperoni. Scarcity means less trust, less opportunity, lower performance, and lower growth. That's small.

The bigger leader brings an abundance mindset. How do we inspire and involve everyone together to make more and bigger pies? More varied types? A veritable feast! More than we could ever eat! (Can you tell I love pizza? Predictable Jersey girl.)

Offer learning and engagement opportunities for employees. You might experiment with lunch-and-learn sessions, coffee chat sessions, or times dedicated to matters on people's minds, whether it be their well-being or something happening externally that's affecting them. I established my Connection Circles program in 2020 as one of my primary culture initiatives to facilitate greater access to relationships across the work environment—to lay the seeds for potential relationships to grow that might not otherwise have happened. This program was also designed to help expand diverse perspectives for leaders across my organization. Five people in a group were assigned to two executives, meeting with them once a month for six months. This was intended to create connections and ideally build relationships that might lead to mentorship and sponsorship.

Sponsors and mentors are key to enabling people throughout their career. Mentors interact with and build a relationship to support the individual and their aspirations, whereas sponsors advocate for an individual—oftentimes without the individual even knowing—because of their standout experiences with that person. Whenever I hosted Connection Circles, I made participation in the program completely optional. Both senior executives and the employees assigned to them tackled many internal and external topics—from the latest organizational restructuring to a competitor's most recent product announcements to the morning's headlines—head-on. The groups got comfortable with one another and enjoyed forming these new diverse relationships. Some of the executives even went on to champion several individuals for promotions and exciting new assignments, while many of the participants developed long-lasting professional relationships across their Connection Circle.

Communicate how you're embracing equity. Equity to me is about fairness, and fair does not mean equal. People may be paid differently due to a variety of factors—skills, responsibilities, experience. Everyone on the team might not be considered for that same promotion, given where they are in their career trajectory. But if you are consistently promoting people who have fewer skills or less experience because you see their "potential," then you might be exhibiting a familiarity bias—promoting people who remind you of yourself earlier in your career, for instance. But this has a negative effect on your team's morale. Our employees expect us to display a comprehensive point of view on equity whether it relates to pay, benefits, opportunities for development and advancement, healthcare access, or otherwise, and be consistent with it. Your responsibility is not just to profess your commitment to belonging and equity and inclusion, but to practice it. I've found it helpful to regularly communicate with people outside my immediate circle, which always required spending substantive time with them. This increased their trust in me, so many grew comfortable with giving me feedback on any given issue, including those related to equity.

In 2020, I also established my Candid Conversations series as a key culture initiative, establishing a platform for open communications, for enhanced understanding, and ideally for learning. This program was catalyzed by the pandemic and the social and racial justice issues in the world, alongside feedback from employees wanting to discuss topics outside of our direct line of work. The series began with a focus on the Black community and a consideration of what it meant to be a Black leader in the corporate world. In a subsequent session, we addressed our communities' relationships with law enforcement, bringing in outside experts as well as employees who either had once served in law enforcement or had a member of their immediate family currently serving. While every one of the sixteen sessions I did received strong engagement and positive feedback, I found one particularly groundbreaking. It was on the topic of religion. Several employees on my panel had different religious backgrounds, including Islam, Christianity, Hinduism, Zoroastrianism, and Judaism. One example of an *aha!* moment that came to life during this conversation was feedback on the company's annual branded holiday/ Christmas ornament at the end of the year. Employees voted on the design and managers often presented the ornaments to others. During the Candid Conversation on religion, one of the participants asked, "For those of us who are not Christian or don't celebrate Christmas, what are we going to do with an ornament?" My eyes widened as it dawned on me that I had a blind spot here. I'd never even thought about this issue because of my own perspective as a Catholic. I'd assumed ornaments were as common and seasonal as a pair of winter gloves. That was a big wow for me: Why would you even want an ornament if you had no tree to hang it on?

Through the Candid Conversations series, we tackled tough issues across many areas, constituencies, and stakeholders: veterans, women, global employees, community leaders, and other groups. This is one of the initiatives I was most proud of as CEO, because it created an environment where it was safe to have such conversations at work—which often led to mini sessions involving smaller teams cascading across the organization. Every one of these sessions helped develop wider perspectives for all who experienced them. Listening and learning became embedded in our organization's culture.

If these inclusive practices seem out of reach for now, take heart in BetterUp's finding that the "presence of a single ally on the team, someone who demonstrated fair and inclusive behavior amidst exclusion from other team members, prevented the negative consequences of social exclusion." In the BetterUp research, this was just a team member who tossed the ball an equal number of times. By being fair and dependable, single leaders working within their circles of control can have a tremendous impact on the workforce's experience.

Remember, the reason leaders should focus on fostering a sense of belonging is to address an essential need of the workforce *to accomplish the work of the organization*. Pointing your workforce toward the purpose of the organization powerfully unites your people across the seemingly infinite and ever-changing dimensions of identities.

Lead Bigger by Prioritizing Well-Being

- Does your organization measure feelings of belonging? Do you notice any variation in belonging across certain groups of employees? What might you do to raise the level for those left behind?

- What skills, training, or coaching do you or your leaders need to prioritize well-being in the workforce? What boundaries do you need to establish around leaders' roles?

- Recall the statistic that 84 percent of workers say their workplace has contributed to at least one mental health challenge. How might *your* team/organization contribute to your workforce's mental health challenges? What could change to alleviate that?

- Which of the tactics at the end of the chapter most resonate with you (and which don't)? Which could you realistically implement in your personal or organization-wide leadership?

DEMYSTIFYING UNCONSCIOUS BIAS
BEAUTY BIAS AND LOOKISM

B ias is an inclination toward or preference for something, and it impacts all pillars of leading bigger—the work, workforce, and workplace. You might recall the term from statistics, where bias is a distortion you watch for, which can otherwise invalidate your results. Bias doesn't necessarily equate to prejudice—most people think it refers to an unfair feeling or dislike of someone or some group—but it can. Some hear the word *bias* and expect to be accused of outright racism.

In fact, bias isn't necessarily negative; it can be as benign as a preference for scrambled eggs or eggs sunny side up. In *The Leader's Guide to Unconscious Bias,* my coauthors and I wrote: "To be human is to have bias. If you were to say, 'I don't have bias,' you'd be saying your brain isn't functioning properly!" It's totally normal to have biases—and your biases span both those you're conscious of and those that are unconscious, often called implicit biases.

The challenge is that bias influences our judgment because it has an effect on how we perceive something. And because it influences our judgment, it can create a ripple effect in our behaviors, words, and decisions. Leaders must pay particular attention to bringing to light unconscious biases that might be negatively impacting our team members. Once these are revealed, we can make more rational, intentional decisions that better reflect reality, increasing the odds of our success.

Bias affects all our senses. Although there are many ways to categorize our senses, for our purposes, let's touch on the five basic human ones: sight, hearing, smell, taste, and feeling. From a hearing perspective, we're all susceptible to auditory illusions like the McGurk effect, where we'll hear a sound differently depending on the way the speaker moves their mouth. As for taste, how many of us have been in situations where an unfamiliar food is put in front of us, and the person serving says, "I'm not going to tell you what it is until you taste it, because you won't try it [because you'll be biased]." For smell, there's a famous fruit in Asia called the durian, which some would say smells like old socks. When you're presented with a durian to eat, you're always told to disregard its smell, because it tastes much better than you'd expect. (As an aside, I can say that I tried it once. The taste was pretty good, but not enough for me conquer my aversion to the odor.) From a tactile perspective, many people have a bias for certain types of fabrics based on the way they feel. Some people prefer cotton, others leather or bamboo or nylon. Softer, more breathable material is the best option, according to many.

The most dominant and valued sense we have is the sense of sight. We gather up to 80 percent of our impressions through our sight. Consider the popular American singing competition, *The Voice*, which premiered back in 2011 and now has expanded to numerous countries around the world. The show's approach to first-round auditions, isolating the sense of hearing without the bias of sight, is one of the favorite elements of the competition. Judges hear the performer with their backs to the stage so they can focus solely on the quality of the voice. Their reactions at the "chair turn" moment are an entertaining example of the dissonance between the expectations created by what they hear and then their surprise at what they see. The shock on the judge's faces, often coupled with a comment such as "You don't look like you sound," illustrates the power of visual bias.

Many women will understand how much expectations shift when they begin to show a pregnancy. In my initial sales job, I was surprised at how, as I grew more visibly pregnant, it affected the way people treated me. Some clients expressed their empathy, while others wrote me off because they felt that soon I wouldn't be around, given my impending maternity leave—to them, our relationship wasn't worth developing. While my pregnancy didn't play into *my* thoughts about how I would interact with my customers, it evoked different reactions from different people because it was visible.

Because so many of our perceptions and biases come from what we see, we're going to explore the impact of visual bias, also known as beauty bias, lookism, or "pretty privilege." This type of bias is by and large legal (unless it's tied to specific anti-discrimination and hate crime laws) and is even openly encouraged in certain industries and roles. The tide may be beginning to turn, as several U.S. states are beginning to ban weight discrimination.

You may be familiar with many cognitive biases already, including recency bias (our preference for the latest information we've encountered), the anchoring effect (our preference for the first information we're presented with), confirmation bias (our preference for information that confirms what we already believe), or in-group bias (our preference for people who are similar to ourselves). This section won't go into an exhaustive exploration of all these unconscious biases, but will rather focus on how a single, often overlooked bias may be affecting how we lead.

Beauty Bias at Work

I was once asked in an interview which virtue I thought was the most overrated. This was an easy question to answer. For me, that was the virtue of beauty, because there is not one standard view, nor should there be, of what is beautiful.

Beauty standards are neither timeless nor universal, even those once thought to be common across the world. For instance, in certain communities in Asia, Africa, South America, and Russia, researchers found that women preferred more "feminine" looking male faces, and in Namibia, women preferred men with shorter legs, versus the lankier Western ideal. Same with the ideal of straight white teeth: various Southeast Asian, East Asian, and Oceanic cultures have practiced teeth blackening throughout their histories. Beauty is truly in the eye of the beholder, culture by culture, person by person. But because of that, we all gravitate toward people we consider attractive, however we define it, and that influences how we hire, promote, and lead our workforce:

- More attractive men earn 9 percent more than their less attractive peers; more attractive women earn 4 percent more.

- Less attractive people are less likely to be hired and more likely to be fired.

- Attractive people are thought to be "more sociable, healthy, successful, honest, and talented."

Beauty bias manifests in many ways, including preferences regarding tattoos, piercings, dress, makeup, hairstyles, and grooming. Bigger leaders must strive to counter the beauty bias in themselves and in others. Let's discuss two of the most harmful biases: heightism and weightism.

Men are most susceptible to height bias. Taller men are perceived to be more successful, confident, and powerful—more like leadership material. Think of the words used around smaller-statured men, slurs like the Napoleon complex or the "little man" syndrome, which are extremely derogatory and are rooted in height bias. Malcolm Gladwell famously revealed in *Blink* that 14.5 percent of U.S. men are six feet or over, but that number leaps to 58 percent among CEOs of Fortune 500 companies. Women face some height bias, though in different ways. Smaller-statured women aren't penalized as much as smaller-statured men, but taller women are perceived as intimidating, threatening, and aggressive.

Let's touch on weight. As you're probably aware, there's a stigma attached to having a bigger body. In the workplace, people who are heavier are viewed

Who is more
attractive?

Who is most
successful?

Who has more
potential?

Who is the
better leader?

as less conscientious, less agreeable, less emotionally stable, and less extroverted, and they are seen as having less potential than their peers of "normal" weight. Women are much more susceptible to weight bias and stigma: An increase in each unit of BMI represents a decrease of 1.83 percent in hourly wages. For men, the weight stigma is inverse: Men who have a lower weight are perceived as less powerful and capable. Bigger men are perceived more positively than bigger women. This aspect of beauty bias has led to a culture of dieting and fat-shaming in America and other cultures.

The other aspect of this beauty bias is its relationship to mental health and overall wellness. Aside from opioid addiction, eating disorders are the number one mental health killer. One in five people who have an eating disorder will die from it, and contrary to gender stereotypes, a quarter of people who have eating disorders are men. It affects people's mental health, their wellness, and their ability to be productive and contributing members of society.

Body inclusivity is "a movement that promotes acceptance of all bodies, regardless of size, shape, skin tone, gender, and physical abilities." The more someone is worried about how they look and how they're being perceived at work, the less attention they have for the work itself. They're not operating at their highest capability. The discussion about celebrating body diversity and ensuring body inclusivity in workplace practices continues to grow in relevance and importance.

The Future of Beauty Bias

During the pandemic, many of us were unable to be in proximity together. Which, in some ways, better leveled the playing field for lookism. One of the reasons why women and people of color enjoyed hybrid/remote work was the reduced pressure to look a certain way, including clothing, hair, makeup, or jewelry. This was also true of others who preferred to dress more comfortably (at least with part of their body) in virtual interactions. The wearing of masks also temporarily defanged this beauty bias.

As we moved on from that period of time, how the workforce physically shows up has now evolved from "I'm expected to dress and look this way" to "I'm going to choose to dress and look this way." Leaders need to be cognizant that people may literally be showing up differently today than they did just a few years ago. For decades, Black women have contended with bias against their natural hair texture, but since the pandemic, a quarter of Black women are more comfortable with their natural hair at work. I believe this is in part due to a cultural awakening people are having about what is both important and authentic. As of this writing, twenty-three states have enacted the CROWN ("Creating a Respectful and Open World for Natural Hair") Act, a law that prohibits race-based hair discrimination. We can expect to see more laws to protect diversity in physical appearance in the future, which inclusive leaders must be extremely mindful of as they consider their own behaviors and those around them.

How to Combat Unconscious Bias at Work

Any time one person can make a decision about another, it's subject to affinity bias, beauty bias, and lookism. Audit your processes and your key decisions when you promote, hire, and fire somebody. Technology and AI can help tackle this bias of sight: using software to screen résumés based on keywords, not on somebody's picture or their name. But we must be vigilant in how we develop and apply AI, as it is subject to bias itself.

Have you ever done a "stare and compare"? Put up the profile pictures of your board, your senior executive team, the engineering managers, the speakers at a conference you're planning, etc. Do you notice anything? Do you see any evidence of beauty bias and lookism? I've encouraged various partners to do this simple assessment. In one case, everyone looked young. In another, a disproportionate number of people had straight blond hair. Another time, it appeared that every person came out of a couture magazine (and this wasn't in the fashion industry). Remember that our dominant sense is our sight. Perhaps that's where the saying "You cannot be what you cannot see" came from?

The key here, just as in so many things, is to have different kinds of people engaged in the important talent decisions. This is not to say that every decision must be made by committee; if that was so, nothing would ever get done. But ask: What critical decisions shouldn't rely just on one person? Because it's not fair to expect one person to overcome all their biases, no matter how inclusive they may be.

Vital points in your workforce processes include the selection vs. the rejection of people, the inclusion vs. the exclusion of people, the performance vs. the potential of people, as well as how the organization is governed. If there is homogeneity, you'll be more vulnerable to unconscious bias that may inhibit positive change. Best practices include panel interviews, different types of skills-based reviews/assessments, and checks and balances in your decision-making.

Our human inclination is to group things to reduce cognitive complexity. This includes people. Some of those generalizations are based on reality, but some are not. Complex factors—neurological, societal, personal—drive us toward our biases. It takes conscious intention to be the bigger leader.

CHAPTER SIX

DIMENSIONALITY

EXPAND YOUR

UNDERSTANDING OF PEOPLE

Leading bigger acknowledges many more aspects of diversity that come into play in the work setting. These nuances of the identity of our people may seem unfamiliar or uncomfortable to you. Inclusive leaders tap into their curiosity, developing empathy and demonstrating care to elevate everyone's growth and performance.

A key part of our humanity is *intersectionality,* a term originated in 1989 by Columbia Law School professor Kimberlé Crenshaw. She coined it in a legal context to describe the multidimensionality of Black women's oppression, which was "greater than the sum" of racism or sexism considered separately. Reflecting more than two decades later, she said: "Intersectionality is a lens through which you can see where power comes and collides, where it interlocks and intersects. It's not simply that there's a race problem here, a gender problem here, and a class or LGBTQ problem there. Many times that framework erases what happens to people who are subject to all of these things."

Intersectionality underscores the fact that each of us is not just one thing. I like to use the word *dimensionality* to reflect the different qualities and attributes we each have, so we don't oversimplify any person's identity. Dimensionality helps us understand these characteristics, while intersectionality reflects the fact that these dimensions, which come together uniquely for each of us, are what makes us the individuals we are. Resisting the desire to categorize individuals or groups of people, using a checkbox on a form to lump them into a class, becomes both a challenge and an opportunity. We tend to apply categories and labels to conceptualize things, which puts us at risk of binary thinking: You are Black or you aren't; you are a veteran or you aren't; you are neurodiverse or you aren't; you live on the West Coast or you don't. We must resist the binary, as it results in overgeneralizations and overarching assumptions about people.

If I use myself as an example, some aspects of my identity, such as my gender, ethnicity, and generation, seem obvious, largely because anyone can see them. In addition to these attributes, I have other given traits, such as my place of birth and my position in my family. But these dimensions only scratch the surface of who I am—and who I am is relevant to what I do, how I do it, and importantly, why I do what I do.

I prefer to look at these characteristics of our identity across two categories: *inherent* and *acquired*. Inherent dimensions are fixed elements of our identities: our race and culture, our place of origin, our sexual orientation, our citizenship status, our gender identity, any disabilities we may have, and so forth. These are at the heart of who we are.

In my case, inherent aspects of my identity are certainly key. Though I was born in the Midwest part of the United States, I was raised in New Jersey and because of that have a certain directness in my leadership style and overall personality. I'm also the child of immigrants, so I have a clear sense of how to think flexibly and take another's perspective, skills born out of an expectation that I learn to fit in.

We also have dimensions of our identity that are *acquired* (developed over time and often chosen). As adults, we can influence and change these dimensions, although in our earlier years, they are largely shaped

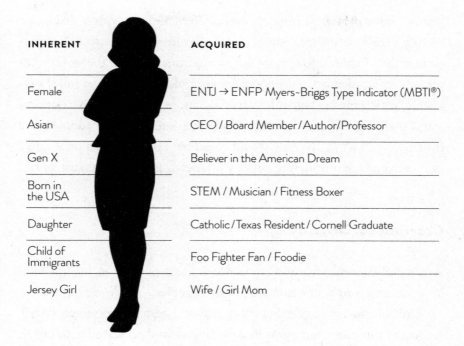

INHERENT	ACQUIRED
Female	ENTJ → ENFP Myers-Briggs Type Indicator (MBTI®)
Asian	CEO / Board Member / Author / Professor
Gen X	Believer in the American Dream
Born in the USA	STEM / Musician / Fitness Boxer
Daughter	Catholic / Texas Resident / Cornell Graduate
Child of Immigrants	Foo Fighter Fan / Foodie
Jersey Girl	Wife / Girl Mom

by others, such as our parents, our teachers, other authority figures, the media, books, and so forth. Identity factors along this dimension include our role/profession, our opinions, our political points of view, our current geographic home, and so forth. Some elements, like personality type or religious affiliation, lie somewhere in between inherent and acquired.

Acquired aspects of identity can especially rival inherent ones in how we show up in the world. A friend once narrowly introduced me as an engineer to a group of high-powered professional women that included doctors, founders, and corporate executives. It was so interesting to see how that positioning changed the social dynamics toward me in the group. Of course I was treated kindly by these women, but it was clear that on some level, they believed me to be beneath them, given their tone and deliberate over-simplification of the discussion. Bigger leaders should resist the explicit or implicit urge to put people in categories that could inhibit greater connection.

Certain aspects of our identities—including race, gender, and disability status—have profound impacts on our lives and are widely discussed among experts and those who share similar lived experiences. The purpose of this chapter is to explore *additional* dimensions of the workforce's identity that leaders often overlook. For example, disabilities are not always visible, which means bigger leaders have more to work to do to understand their workforce's challenges and situations. Bigger leaders have a broad view of what diversity is and could be. We will touch on a range of dimensions of our identity, but by no means is this an exhaustive set.

Generational Diversity

As mentioned earlier, many of our dimensions are not chosen, but inherent. Your age and your generation are prime examples—they're simply facts.

Current and future members of the up-and-coming workforce, Gen Z represent the most demographically diverse and educated generation yet. Racial and ethnic minorities make up almost 50 percent of Gen Z.

This younger workforce has different expectations and are opening our eyes to alternative perspectives of inclusion. Additionally, most Gen Z workers believe that financial and childcare responsibilities should be shared by partners, a significant demographic shift discussed further in chapter 10. They are helping us see that childcare and eldercare responsibilities are more than just personal and social issues; they're economic and business imperatives that modern leaders and organizations must address.

Gen Zers generally believe the role of government should be more significant in society, which presents an opportunity for public and private partnerships. At the same time, global national division has created a growing mistrust of the government from people across multiple generations. The workforce has expectations that corporations should prioritize, helping drive progress in equity, inclusion, and sustainability/climate change. Corporate sustainability and social responsibility ultimately affect employee retention. Nine out of ten Gen Zers and millennials are already engaged in efforts to protect the planet, either through individual or collective action.

Let's highlight a few data points that might challenge your perceptions of the oldest generations in the workforce today.

- Beginning in 2024, nearly 25 percent of the workforce is fifty-five and older.

- People aged fifty-five and older are the fastest-growing segment of the American workforce.

- Boomers did as much job-hopping in their twenties as millennials did at that age.

We are currently living and working in an environment where we have five generations in the workforce. This has resulted in a couple of age-old (no pun intended) challenges,

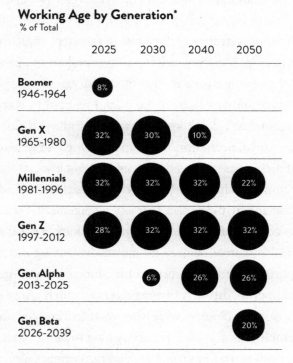

Working Age by Generation*
% of Total

	2025	2030	2040	2050
Boomer 1946-1964	8%			
Gen X 1965-1980	32%	30%	10%	
Millennials 1981-1996	32%	32%	32%	22%
Gen Z 1997-2012	28%	32%	32%	32%
Gen Alpha 2013-2025		6%	26%	26%
Gen Beta 2026-2039				20%

*Not adjusted for population size
Working age defined as ages 15-64 per OECD data (data.oecd.org)

Most common is ageism. People from younger generations some-times feel that their elders need to move on and get out of the way, exhibiting a disdain of sorts coupled with little respect. And mem-bers of older generations may feel that younger people haven't had to go through the trenches and haven't lived enough to know or make demands. Gen Zers sometimes use stereotypical phrases like *Okay, boomer* and coined the Karen label. Those from the older generations sometimes comment that younger people are spoiled and oftentimes lazy, having grown up with participation awards. They often characterize those younger than they are as not willing to put in the work or make longer-term commitments.

When it comes to generational and age diversity, you can unleash great team dynamics if you lead in a way that eliminates judgment. Judgment is the enemy of inclusion. Seek opportunities to bring people of different ages together. You can learn a lot as part of an intergenerational team—and they're more fun to be part of!

One of the most effective techniques to facilitate these dynamics is two-way mentoring. Most assume the senior person in age and tenure will mentor the younger person, but the value goes both ways. Given that my organization was all over the map, I wanted to start a regular blog for my team, but I didn't know how. I didn't have a clue about the different styles and expectations between blogging and writing an email or a personal note on my beloved Post-its, so I got a social media coach who was far younger than me. His guidance helped me find my voice and get comfortable with the fact that any engagement—whether posi-tive, negative, or neutral—is the objective. It took me a good six months with lots of trial and error before I hit my stride. During this time, I also mentored my coach on his career and life objectives, and our relation-ship was meaningful. Through this experience, which spanned nearly a decade of my career, I blogged weekly to my team, and for nine consec-utive years, employees at AT&T voted my blog to be the best. What I'm most proud of is how this approach helped me connect with my people across the generations in a more personal way. They got to know my children and dogs and watched them grow; they experienced my travels secondhand; and when we did get together in person, it was clear they felt more connected and committed to me—not just as a leader, but as a person who cared about them, our culture, our customers, and our business. My blogging enabled us to experience and reflect on our time together in unique and memorable ways, all while delivering excellent performance together as a team.

Given the short supply of skilled workers, we can't afford to fall into the idea that employees fifty-five and older should just retire and go away. Many organizations value the young and the fresh and are concerned that institutional knowledge and experience don't yield breakthroughs. This is not simply a paradigm of young leaders. No doubt you've encountered older leaders who seem to devalue more tenured workers, not even considering the possibility of equipping these employees with new skills and developing them. Leaders should reconsider their people who are retirement eligible and have much to offer but are not being provided with career growth. Institutional knowledge is also vital to any business's transformation and future success. As the *Harvard Business Review* puts it, "Older workers bring an extra level of emotional intelligence to the workplace; additionally, older workers reduce costs because they are less likely to leave voluntarily and have lower turnover rates on teams they supervise. Older workers are crucial to creating environments with knowledge sharing and mentoring, and studies suggest that their presence strengthens group cohesion, collaboration, and resiliency."

Linguistic Diversity

A common experience for Black and Asian Americans is to be told, "You're so articulate" or "You speak really well!" It's certainly happened to me many times in my career, and I've often wondered if I looked different whether I'd still receive this type of feedback.

Linguistic bias blends the bias of two senses together: sight and sound. For example, just the sight of an Asian face makes listeners hear the English of the speaker as more accented, even if the person who is talking is a native speaker of English. The brain is almost warping sound to fit our existing biases.

Despite the fact that non-native speakers of English around the globe outnumber native English speakers three to one, research has found that certain accents and linguistic differences hurt your paycheck, depending on where you are geographically and in what setting. According to the BBC, "A particular status is attached to English that sounds as if it comes from countries that are wealthy, majority white and mostly monolingual. According to this limited view, multilingual countries like Nigeria and Singapore have less 'legitimate' and desirable forms of English (even though English is an official language in both). Globally, the most respected types of English are varieties such as British, American, and Australian." We value non-native accents similarly: European-accented English is often deemed sophisticated, while Asian-, African-, or Middle Eastern–accented English is perceived as unpleasant or challenging.

Here's some more revealing data about our linguistic biases:

- Societies and cultures around the world have biases against or for certain ways of speaking. Journalist Sarah Todd wrote in *Quartz*, "In Japan, the Tōhoku regional accent is stereotypically associated with laziness and provinciality; in Brazil, Northeastern accents are considered socially inferior." In the United States, rural or Southern accents are often stigmatized.

- People with strong regional accents face a wage penalty of 20 percent compared to those who speak a standard accent.

- Black Americans who speak with a mainstream dialect tend to earn more money than those who speak African American Vernacular English.

Part of what's happening here is the manifestation of affinity bias, the human tendency to like people who are similar to oneself. Additionally, it does take more brainpower for us to understand unfamiliar accents. But as with all negative biases, linguistic preferences can lead us to ascribe false meaning to people, to the point that people unconsciously assume non-native speakers of English are less trustworthy, competent, credible, or intelligent, without any factual basis.

We should be cautious that what we're unfamiliar with doesn't fuel unintended biases in our thoughts, our assessments of someone, or the way we choose to work with them. I purposefully coach myself not to leap to conclusions, not to let my mind wander, and not to discount what I'm hearing when I become less patient with someone. As a Jersey girl, I'll admit a tendency to do so when someone is speaking at a pace that is significantly slower than mine!

Personality Type

One of the areas of diversity where our tendencies can get the better of us is in personality type and expression. We inevitably gravitate toward people who are like us because it feels good and it's comfortable—another example of affinity bias. Comfort, however, is not the objective in today's dynamic marketplace. Comfort doesn't spark innovation or provide the growth and debate we need to ensure that ideas are sustainable and well thought out. In the wise words of Brené Brown, "Integrity is choosing courage over comfort." We need to resist comfort at times, especially in building connections and developing meaningful relationships with people.

Many of us have gone through a litany of personality tests throughout our careers—Myers Briggs, Enneagram, Birkman, Hogan—and whatever the framework, rarely is one personality type better than another. We should be mindful of when certain personality types may dominate a team or conversation. Two of the most well-known dimensions of personality are extroversion/introversion. Let's look at a few surprising data points:

- According to HubSpot, "A meta-analysis of 35 studies that surveyed 4,000 salespeople found almost zero correlation . . . between extraversion and sales performance." Introverts perform just as well in sales roles.

- "Whereas just 50% of the general population is extroverted, 96% of managers and executives display extroverted personalities. And the higher you go in a corporate hierarchy, the more likely you are to find highly extroverted individuals," according to researchers Francesca Gino, David A. Hofmann, and Adam Grant (who we'll hear from in an interview later in this book).

- Introverted CEOs exceeded investor expectations more often than extroverts, in a study of 900 CEOs.

Oftentimes we misinterpret intention when someone's delivery is different from how we would have handled the situation. Their communication style is less appealing to us because it's not what we're comfortable with. This feeds an anchoring bias—if somebody who's similar to you says something, you're going to latch onto that view. Then your confirmation bias shows up, where you'll be less apt to hear from somebody else who might have a different approach or style yet have very important points to make. We're all subject to the risks of drifting toward certain personality styles and types that we're more comfortable with. Throughout my career, I've observed repeatedly that confidence is not correlated to competence.

Neurodiversity

People with autism, attention deficit hyperactivity disorder (ADHD), dyslexia, learning disabilities, and other conditions are grouped under the term *neurodiverse*. Overall, one in seven people are neurodivergent (though this number depends on how neurodiversity is defined); specifically, 10 percent of the global adult population has dyslexia,

5 percent has ADHD, 6 percent have dyspraxia, and 1 to 2 percent have autism.

Neurodiverse people are frequently overlooked or even purposefully excluded, and many workplaces don't implement measures to accommodate their needs. Half of UK managers said they would not hire neurodivergent talent. To use autism as an example:

- "The unemployment rate of autistic college graduates in the U.S. is as high as 85%, while 46% of employed autistic adults are overeducated or overqualified for their roles," according to *Fast Company*.

- Yet research finds that autistic professionals are generally more productive than the average employee. JPMorgan Chase found that their autistic employees were 48 percent faster and 92 percent more productive than neurotypical employees.

As inclusive leaders, we should evaluate our own perceptions and perhaps even biases against neurodivergence. With any lack of empathy and understanding, neurodiverse people—especially anyone on the autism spectrum—can find themselves being harshly judged or even bullied at work.

In my career, I've had neurodiverse team members with conditions such as dyslexia and ADHD. In these situations, I've developed strong enough relationships with these individuals such that they told me about their neurodivergence. I secured the accommodations they needed to get the job done—whether it involved giving them extensions on projects or making sure our conversations and tasks were segmented into bite-size chunks of time, with notes that could be referred to afterward. People who are neurologically diverse have much to offer the workforce, including problem-solving using different thinking patterns that may spark innovation or capture errors others overlook. As bigger leaders, we must foster a workplace and culture that supports all ways of listening, learning, collaborating, and contributing.

Religious Diversity

I once attended an executive conference in Asia that was planned by a U.S.-based team with little to no global experience. This was a multiday conference with around-the-clock content, so meals and snacks were important. Unfortunately, on day one, it became clear that no one had taken into account the fact that many of the attendees were vegetarian, given their religious beliefs. The only food available to them was plain rice, and those who were vegetarian felt excluded during what was intended to be an important strategic leadership conference. This misstep inadvertently sent a message to a group of us that something as basic as our dietary needs had not even been considered. However, with every fumble, there is an opportunity to improve and grow. Major changes were made, and from day two on, the conference served platters of vegetarian food during mealtimes. And you can bet that every person on the planning team and those who were paying attention never made that mistake again.

Religion has chronically been a taboo topic in the workplace. About a third of people in the United States view religion as the single most uncomfortable topic to discuss there. Of course, this view is long outdated, as our religious and spiritual beliefs are vital to who we are. I once worked for someone who was a practicing Roman Catholic, and he made it known that he went to mass every day at 7:30 a.m., including on our business trips. He wasn't judgy about it, but people knew not to schedule a meeting with him or try to reach him during that time. He earned respect because of his openness about his faith.

Some simple ways to be more aware of religious diversity:

- Be careful referencing God, Jesus Christ, Allah, or any other prominent religious figure in professional settings. Examples include, "Can I get an amen?" and "Let's start this meeting/meal with a prayer." I myself have had to break my habit of saying, "God works in mysterious ways," when something serendipitous happens. If I'm with friends, I'll use this expression, but in a work environment, it's less appropriate.

- For large, mandatory meetings, check religious calendars for conflicts. This takes just a quick internet search, but inclusive leaders need to create an environment where people are comfortable letting you know about an issue like this. You can't possibly know everything, nor do you want to walk on eggshells. In an open environment, employees know it's okay to raise these concerns. Of course no situation is perfect, and if you must schedule something that conflicts with an important day—acknowledge it, own it, apologize for it, and provide a work-around for those impacted. And please be sure not to inadvertently penalize those who don't attend due to personal priorities.

- Create a focus on an interfaith employee community. Establish and sponsor a specific employee resource group whose members are representative of multiple religions and geographies. Charter them to help raise awareness and advance understanding of different religions from all around the world.

Political Diversity

Acquired traits evolve and are often consciously chosen: what food we like to eat, where we like to vacation, what genre we enjoy reading, and what media we consume. And one of these chosen dimensions is politics.

Politics are based on differences. Thus they can be innately polarizing. And in today's hypersensitized, divisive environment, a specific challenge arises for bigger leaders: How do you create a culture of inclusion, one in which you maintain professionalism, civility, and respect? And how do you address different political points of view with equal voice and balance, with the objective of trying to minimize tension, lower stress levels, and have healthy, humble interactions of compromise and collaboration? In other words, how can you make politics less polarizing in the workplace you control?

Some data points:

- Research conducted by the Society for Human Resource Management shows that 95 percent of U.S. employees have been involved in polarizing workplace discussions, whether as participants, bystanders, or managers.

- And 44 percent of employees have avoided coworkers because of their political beliefs, a clear demonstration of how mishandling this dimension of the workforce can negatively impact the work of the organization.

As Thomas Jefferson, no stranger to heated politics, wrote back in 1800: "I never considered a difference of opinion in politics, in religion, in philosophy, as cause for withdrawing from a friend." Politics have become so supercharged that liberals, conservatives, *and* moderates fear that their beliefs will have a negative impact on their career:

- According to the Cato Institute, a libertarian think tank, "Nearly a third of employed Americans say they personally are worried about missing out on career opportunities or losing their job if their political opinions become known." This finding is consistent across the political spectrum, race, and income level.

- Younger people and more educated people are most concerned, again across political affiliation.

As bigger leaders, how do we handle this? We must be intentional about what we say, validating the feelings of all people and not discounting them. Embracing multidimensionality in the workplace includes respecting people's politics. In the workplace, disagreements are meant to enable discussions of diverse perspectives on all topics—with a focus on how they relate to the work at hand. If an issue is challenging or sensitive, we must be sure to have the view of our stakeholders as primary. They are, after all, why our business exists.

Perhaps the most difficult thing for many leaders is accepting that we cannot pick sides. We must always put our individual perspectives and position aside as we seek to understand others. Our responsibility is to lead all the people, not just those we agree with. We should not confuse our values with differing ideologies. Ideologies can be formed based on religious, political, cultural, or other reasons. Performance through powerful purpose and aligned values is our focus as bigger leaders—not the endless range of ideologies that naturally exist across a diverse population.

Here are the tactics that have helped me navigate politics in and out of the office:

Do not ignore it. Your people want to hear from you. They expect to hear from you. If you say nothing, they will assume you don't care. If geopolitics or federal, state, or local politics impact your business directly, such as in heavily regulated industries, elaborate on this context for your people so they understand its relevance to your business objectives. You'll need to manage your own emotions on the topic and lean into empathy by acknowledging how people are feeling. This also requires courage. Remember you are commenting as the leader of the business, not as an individual.

Reinforce your business purpose, values, and objectives. When things get heated or you're not sure what to say, affirm your commitment to the purpose and values of your organization. Cite examples where you, your teams, and your company have stepped up to demonstrate your values even when it might not have been the most politically correct thing to do.

Take a global perspective. Even if your company or organization isn't global, you need to be aware of what's happening in geopolitics, as this may be important to your people. They may have relatives or friends in an affected area, or they may even hail from a region of the world where the strife is occurring. Avoid taking an ethnocentric approach to global happenings, embracing a more neutral posture if possible. Ask for insight. Go to your employee groups and get clarity on how to be sensitive to global catastrophes or events. Maintain a diverse network where there can be respectful conversation about varying viewpoints, so that you can remain educated about how to show up and handle hot topics sensitively.

Create a safe environment for dialogue. Whatever the forum may be—a live candid conversation, a panel discussion during a town hall, a talk by an unbiased outside expert—demonstrate to your team that they can engage with one another, even with differing political views. Play the role of arbitrator and scientist, gathering the facts. Ensure that multiple different views can be heard. Don't allow an echo chamber to develop.

Demonstrate vulnerability. This is best done with you and your leadership team first, to set the tone of acceptability and openness. Where there might be confusion around words, behaviors, and actions, make sure to involve HR and legal professionals. Topics such as minimum wage debates, for instance, can touch on labor laws related to employees' right to discuss their pay. Laws vary from country to country and even from state to state. Once you have the legal guardrails clearly in place, you can ask for feedback and multiple points of view. Share your concerns and talk about times you've stumbled—and times you've learned.

Set boundaries and apply consequences. Demand and reinforce respect for the individual, and do not tolerate toxicity. Handle violations against your company values and conduct requirements (including unacceptable words and behaviors) swiftly, with consequences. The repercussions should be clearly conveyed to all employees through both verbal and written communications. Provide a clear code of conduct, making it clear that any violation will result in job loss. One best practice for companies is to have employees review those expectations and consequences every year and verify that they understand them. If the infraction is serious enough, human resources and/or legal should conduct investigations. Document violations of the code of conduct in performance reviews and adjust compensation if needed, or institute requirements for intense training, or if nothing else works, terminate the employee.

You may be tempted to squash political discourse in the workplace. But as much as we fear our political differences, bigger leaders know that "ideologically polarized teams engage in longer, more constructive, competitive and substantively focused but linguistically diverse debates than teams of ideological moderates." Researchers also explain that "Collectively, teams with mixtures of bias that are willing to engage and collaborate can yield superior performance. This reveals a 'silver lining' of political diversity and disagreement in these polarized times. Even as political polarization rises in the U.S. and around the world, if we realize the other side has something worthwhile to say, the arguments become smarter than the participants."

Gender Identity

Without question, Gen Z has brought the discussion of gender identity and fluidity into the mainstream. For example, Pew Research found:

- Over one-third of Gen Z knows someone who uses gender-neutral pronouns.

- Nearly 60 percent of Gen Z believe there should be nonbinary options when identifying somebody's profile or information.

- Globally, 25 percent of Gen Z will change their gender identity at least once in their lifetime.

- Adults under thirty are more likely than older adults to be trans or nonbinary.

- Although the percentage of transgender adults is relatively small, 44 percent of people say they know a trans person, and this percentage has increased rapidly since 2017. Notably, 13 percent say they have a trans coworker.

- In the United States, 26 percent of adults say they personally know someone who goes by gender-neutral pronouns such as *they* instead of *he* or *she,* up from 18 percent in 2018.

Gender identity is a dimension of personal identity that can produce different types of dialogue. At the most basic level, we must respect the individual, every individual. While this may be uncomfortable to some, perhaps based on their ideologies or experiences, as leaders, we are obligated to seek and develop the best talent possible. No group of people should be excluded from this. Pew Research currently finds that "half of Americans say they would feel very or somewhat comfortable using a gender-neutral pronoun to refer to someone if they were asked to do so, while 48% say they would feel very or somewhat uncomfortable doing so. . . . Age and political party are also strongly related to comfort with using gender-neutral pronouns." To build meaningful connections and help all people realize their fullest potential requires that we open not only our arms but our minds and hearts, too.

Veteran Status

Veterans hold a special place in our society. They have stepped up to serve their country, willing to make the ultimate sacrifice of their lives to protect their nation. Once this job is over, their experiences and perspectives can be harnessed in the professional world. Having supported veterans in many of my leadership roles and in my own family, I've learned that transition and assimilation are often challenging. Once surrounded by clear structures, hierarchies, and roles, veterans find that civilian corporate life often lacks all of the above. In the military, it is crystal clear where the power resides and who ultimately owns decisions. These pathways are not always clear in the business world. In addition, if a veteran suffers from PTSD, the reality of their needs may be entirely different.

Veterans represent just over 5 percent of the U.S. workforce. They tend to be employed at higher rates than nonveterans, although they are more likely to be *under*employed.

- Upwards of 20 percent of veterans experience PTSD each year, compared to less than 4 percent of the general population.

- About 59 percent of employers reported that veterans perform "better than" or "much better than" their nonveteran peers, with employers highly valuing veterans' experience and their perseverance.

- Veterans face a stereotype of being unemotional and are less likely to be considered for roles that require interpersonal skills or emotional intelligence. Research found that hiring managers often slot them in roles involving things as opposed to people.

Steve Cannon, CEO of AMB Group and a veteran himself, said in an interview, "The biggest barrier to me is isolation. . . . [Veterans] come from a cohort—a platoon, a squadron—and what happens with veterans is that often when they lose that sense of team and support, that can sometimes lead to bad outcomes." A sense of belonging, perhaps in the form of a specific employee resource group, is critical for veteran success, just as much as it is for nonveterans.

In this chapter, I've highlighted a few underexplored dimensions of our workforce, but the reality is that an infinite number of dimensions form each of us as individuals, and no two people hold the same combination. In fact, what is characteristic of an individual today will assuredly change over time. This equation isn't solvable. To deal with this complexity, bigger leaders both embrace known dimensions and stay open to unfamiliar ones. In the powerful words of organizational consultant Margarita Sarmiento, "An organization's impact can only be as strong as the willingness of its people to take on the perspectives of others."

Leading Bigger by Embracing Dimensionality

- What dimensions are currently included in your organization's view of diversity?

- Which dimensions have formal programs, initiatives, or executive focus/sponsorship?

- After reflecting on this chapter, which dimensions of your workforce have been neglected?

- Which dimensions are emerging, changing, or becoming more relevant?

- What could you or your organization do to be more inclusive of those dimensions? Do you have goals for your actions? How would you track them?

CHAPTER SEVEN

VITALITY

INVIGORATE THE EMPLOYEE EXPERIENCE

The traditional HR term *employee lifecycle* presumes a fixed beginning and end. Bigger leaders ensure workforce vitality, considering both current and future workforce needs and incorporating the perspectives of employees so they can thrive in their present-day jobs and careers.

The terms *employee lifecycle* and *talent lifecycle* are commonly used by leaders and HR professionals to describe the stages of an employee's journey through the company. I've shied away from the use of the term *lifecycle* because it implies a career is in finite phases. The term suggests the person matters only from hiring through the end of employment— almost like a birth and a death. It reminds me of the words on a poster from high school biology class: *The life cycle of a fruit fly: from egg to larva and pupa to adult!*

I prefer to use *workforce vitality* to convey that your workforce is your "lifeforce." You want your workforce to be perpetually strong, focused, energetic, and future oriented. And especially in today's world, the demands on your workforce are continually evolving. Your team from yesterday may not be the right one for today, and today's team will likely not be the best team for the future.

In my mind, the meaning of vitality is a living energy that is never stagnant, needs continuous renewal, and has the capacity to grow. It balances both what the company needs from the employee *and* what the employee needs from the company. Vitality encourages you to consider more aspects of your people's experience. And vitality necessitates that you consider the different stages of an individual without a beginning or an end and commit to their development and growth.

Workforce vitality requires the bigger leader to consider each career stage both in the interest of the company (employer) and in the eyes of the individual (employee). The Workforce Vitality Framework diagram below depicts employer priorities as attraction, engagement, and separation, while the employee prioritizes interest, contribution, and departure. We separate them here because the motivations of the company and of the individual will differ at points. Because the degree of alignment between the employee and the employer is situational, the bigger leader considers both perspectives. As an example, when the individual no longer works for the company, the bigger leader recognizes the importance of that former employee as a potential promoter or detractor, customer, and even shareholder.

The framework consists of eight elements, which are represented by the circles in the diagram. These are positioning, recruiting, hiring, onboarding, performance development, career development, attrition, and succession planning. The steps are numbered but aren't necessarily linear. A team member may be hired and onboarded to new teams within the same company, for instance. Another may leave the company, then return. The inclusive leader builds the optimal team, which means having the right people in the right roles, for whatever period of time is necessary.

Lead Bigger Workforce Vitality Framework

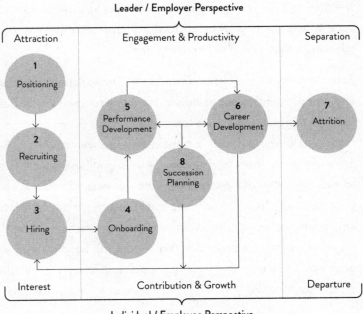

Positioning as an Employer of Choice

Positioning is about attracting talent, starting with understanding where they'll learn about your brand. We harken back to Part 1, where we discussed making sure your brand links to the preferences of your desired customers. Many organizations don't prioritize how they position themselves for their future pool of talent as much as they do for their future customers.

- *Make sure your organizational purpose and values are visible to your desired talent pools.* High-value potential recruits are stake-holders, and ideally they can clearly see that their purpose and values align with yours. For example, if your focus is on exper-tise or innovation, you may want to put your ideas on display via thought leadership in the media. If employee culture is a big differentiator for you, aim for the annual lists of the greatest places to work and the rankings of best-managed companies. Keep an eye on workplace review sites like Glassdoor to make sure you know how your current and former employees are speaking about you in the marketplace.

- *Take the perspective of your employees if they see other companies and brands standing out as having more impact than yours.* Positioning your brand to attract talent does double duty: It's for your future workforce and your current teams. Employees want to feel pride in the company and a sense of belonging and trust. Here's an example. Suppose you're a talented woman and you don't see your company included in a reputable, highly visible list of top employers for women, but your competitors are high up on the list, what might your perception be? And if this happens over and over, would you consider exploring opportunities with those other companies? Putting yourself in her shoes, of course you would!

Recruiting

One of the biggest missteps organizations make is treating candidate recruitment as episodic. They go out to the places where talent might be, physically or digitally, only when they have an immediate or short-term need to hire. Bigger leaders build and sustain relationships in those places or organizations, so that when hiring needs arise, they're already well established as attractive employers.

- *Become a trusted part of the communities you want to recruit from.* It's the relationships that will matter in your time of need, which requires thought and targeting on your part. This means *investment*: a financial/sponsorship commitment, in-kind services, the provision of experts and volunteers to support their objectives, and even formal agreements to hire a specific number of candidates over a period of time.

- *Connect your positioning and recruiting efforts.* Is your messaging landing in the places where you are developing relationships? Don't forget about your "influencers," including the full array of organizations around you. Even in B2B industries, winning affirmation from respected people such as analysts, industry leaders, academic experts, and journalists can go a long way. Think about it from the perspective of the talent you want to hire. Make it easy for them to get to know you.

Hiring

Leaders often regret that they didn't address issues with their poor performers sooner. How about starting all the way back when you first hired those folks who ultimately weren't going to succeed? Think of how this played out from the perspective of the employee who didn't fit. Getting fired can be traumatic and can erode that employee's self-esteem in the working world for years to come. Rarely do hiring managers take equivalent responsibility for their poor selection.

Leading small is hiring for surface characteristics, checking boxes instead of peeling back the candidates' goals and styles of working, making sure they enhance not just the role but the mix already on the team.

- *Don't just follow your gut.* Lots of tools and best practices already exist to help you hire more effectively (hiring panels, skills testing, checking for a match of values and purpose, and so forth), but they are often not put to use. Why? Many managers believe that they're amply capable of selecting the best candidates without these tools and best practices, preferring to go by instinct. Others lean too much on HR for prequalification and screening.

Hiring managers usually want to bring staff on quickly. But as you enter the hiring process, you need to consider the current composition of your team and identify what you are missing.

- **Don't "clone" past employees, your favorite colleagues, or even your-self.** Your team might desperately need someone with a new approach. If the group is composed of fast innovators who struggle to follow through, they might not like someone process-oriented— but that might be exactly what your team needs to succeed.

Onboarding

How many of us have experienced speed bumps when starting a new job? It's two weeks in, and we're still feeling a lingering helplessness, without key tools or access to whom or what we need. We're "going into the office," whether it's virtual or physical, and we're severely underutilized. We haven't been onboarded both figuratively and literally—which is more than just getting your identification badge and turning on your laptop. This is too often a big miss.

Treat onboarding as a way to shape an employee's trajectory, rather than as an afterthought to the hiring process. Onboarding should be separate from the hiring process, although many organizations mistakenly consider them one and the same. A more robust definition of onboarding is the integration of people into your team and onto the learning curve. Does their early experience match the expectations set in the recruiting process?

- **Consider new members in an onboarding phase anywhere from six months to a year, depending on their background and role.** Too many companies skip through this in a month or less, rather than spending the time needed to establish the new employee's sense of belonging.

- **Put into context where that person is in the organization, what their role is, and how they fit into the company's strategy and pur-**

pose. I came from an industry that often feels like you're living in Acronym City and having alphabet soup for lunch every day. Providing a "decoder ring" early on helps the person feel like they haven't landed on an alien planet.

- *Establish camaraderie and connection through assigned buddies, other colleagues who have been recently hired, and/or mentors.* Groups of new hires will stick together throughout their careers if they feel like a team. Mentor relationships that form in the early days of one's career will often be the most formative and enduring.

- *Continuously ask for feedback during this process.* And make it safe for them to tell you what they really think, to establish safety and candor early.

- *Don't forget about your nontraditional workforce.* How do you onboard your gig workers and contractors?

- *Re-onboard internal hires, too.* Too often we progress or promote employees and then just leave them to figure it out. Support them in the same way as you would a new employee.

Bridging to Performance and Career

Once an employee is a full-fledged member of a team, you should focus on two forms of development: *performance* and *career* development. *Performance development* is about ensuring individuals have the skills to do their job and an understanding of how to improve their performance through feedback and evaluation. It's about what they do and can do in their current role.

However, most people care about more than just the current job they have; they're also thinking about their careers more broadly.

Thus *career development* is much bigger, longer term, and more personal.

Many leaders combine the two elements, assuming that "When I'm supporting my employee in their performance on this job, I'm also supportive of their career." More often than not, when managers don't explicitly dedicate time with an employee to discuss their career, such discussion falls to the wayside, because performance in the current role will always be the priority. More and more today, the workforce wants more feedback and wants to know they're moving toward something. Without this, they become uninspired. And over time, without this "itch being scratched," they will seek fulfillment elsewhere.

First let's talk about performance.

Performance Development

Performance development involves everything a leader does to support individuals in unlocking their greater potential by widening their skill set (i.e. expanding their product, technical, and systemic knowledge). The needs of the job may change, so new skills may be called for. Performance development can often be lost on new supervisors, who immediately start managing tasks and focusing on productivity and output before they understand where each person currently stands.

Performance development also means ensuring the group and the individuals hit their objectives together, meeting timelines for the quality and quantity of projects in whatever acceptable manner has been established.

- *Include more people in performance reviews and feedback.* As I've mentioned before, any time a decision rests in one person's hands or is dominated by one person, you run the risk of bias playing a disproportionate role. Inclusive leaders build systemic, structured ways to garner feedback from others about that person. This might mean an easy-to-administer survey developed by HR or more ad hoc but thorough conversations.

- *Make compensation more transparent.* When it comes to pay, I have seen that, unfortunately, bias comes into the picture. Bigger leaders work diligently to ensure pay is directly correlated with performance, all the way up to the board level. Success in the workplace can depend on soft skills like empathy, connection, collaboration, and innovation. How do you eliminate as much subjectivity as possible while also fostering skills that are difficult to measure? Measure performance inclusively with an eye on what matters. I'm a big believer in balancing the what somebody accomplishes with how they accomplish it. When you talk about the how, which is where human skills come in, you can create, sometimes with HR, examples and definitions of what collaboration, communication, ingenuity, innovation, or courage look like.

- *Make sure your bar for success is consistent with the bar your peers and management use.* Some leaders may be more lenient or strict in applying performance management criteria and measurements. As best as you can, establish clear quantitative boundaries. Check with your key counterparts to make sure you're in agreement about what's expected from your people, in terms of both quantitative metrics like key performance indicators and qualitative behaviors like collaboration and creativity.

- *When giving significant feedback, sample at least half a dozen other people with diverse perspectives who have direct experience with your team members.* Getting an accurate reading on a person's human skills is measured in the individual's impact on the group. Human skills clearly do contribute to the person's achievement of goals (the what), but sometimes that's harder to see. But these human skills will almost always show up quickly in feedback from other people (the how).

- *Individualize a growth and development plan.* Not everybody will benefit from the same training program. Not everybody will benefit from the same weekly check-in. Not everybody will benefit from the same development structure or mentoring program. It's up to the bigger leader to work with that individual to figure out what works best with them. Leaders must meet their people where the people need them.

Career Development

An employee's current job is simply a point in that person's overall career. And you must understand and nurture that individual's career aspirations, because performance development is most compelling to an individual when it's linked to their career development. While the former is led by the manager/supervisor, the latter must be led by the individual, because it's that person's career.

- *Don't assume every employee wants a traditional career path.* For some people, career growth means promotion up the proverbial corporate ladder; for some, it's networking or working with emerging technologies. For others, career development means greater compensation, a more exalted title, more power, and a greater chance to contribute. Or it means accolades and achievements, external awards, or milestones like certifications or degrees. Some people may have an "inside job" to do; they feel disorganized, socially anxious, or like an impostor at work every day and want to improve their mindset. The bigger leader recognizes that it is natural for people to want more, and subsequently works with them to understand what that "more" looks like. Support their aspirations by being curious and serving as a sounding board. Remember: your experience is not their experience!

- *Don't assume everyone wants to be in management.* One of the fallacies of career development is the belief that you must become a direct manager to be a leader. I've never believed that. I believe that leadership is a choice, and that you can lead people in any role, because bigger leadership is about nurturing the greatest potential among the people in your purview, in ways they may not have ever thought achievable. You can choose to lead bigger from any seat.

- *Help employees gain allies, coaches, mentors, and sponsors.* Allies support you. Coaches talk *to* you about a specific skill or area. Mentors talk *with* you in a two-way relationship where you can be your full authentic self. Sponsors advocate for you and talk *about* you. Throughout our careers, we need people who fill all four of those roles. Like vocal, athletic, and writing coaches, a professional or career coach focuses on a particular skill or goal. Mentorship empowers growth in both directions. Mentoring relationships can be situational and temporary in nature, or they can be sustained over a period of time. A mentor needs to know their mentee's professional and personal aspirations. Take stock of your mentees and your mentors. Do you observe any homogeneity when you study them side by side? Could you mentor *bigger*? Sponsorship can only be earned. Sponsors have firsthand experience with you; they must know of your performance directly and feel positively about your potential as they talk about you when you're not in the room, positioning you for different and even greater things.

- *Check for exclusion on your part when you coach, mentor, and sponsor employees.* I'm sure all of us have run into (smaller) leaders who sponsor only their friends and people who are just like them. In fact, 71 percent of executives choose protégés of the same gender and race. The bigger leader works hard to move beyond their comfort zone, especially when it comes to sponsorship, because this boosts career development and workforce vitality. Your time and energy are finite resources.

Attrition

Attrition—meaning people leaving your organization—sometimes happens involuntarily for a slate of reasons: performance issues, a failure to meet objectives, a breach of the code of business conduct, an ethics or severe compliance violation. Voluntary separations, on the other hand, involve retiring, changing careers, moving on to other roles outside of your company, or leaving the industry altogether.

- *See if bias is showing up in the separation process.* Are you losing a disproportionate number of people from a certain generation, geographical area, or part of the organization, which may flag an unhealthy work culture? The bigger leader slices and dices that information, correlating it to demographics like gender, race, role, tenure, location, performance, and generation. They seek to understand the trends and the why, then work to get ahead of them to increase the probability of retaining key talent.

- *Use data to locate where opportunities to bolster culture exist.* Couple that data with leading indicators of insight such as employee pulse surveys which tend to be brief and more frequent, along with more formal feedback check-ins with prospective and active employees.

- *Consider former employees as stakeholders.* Just as we want to make strong impressions with potential employees long before they're hired, we want to maintain mutual respect and affinity with employees long after they leave. Former employees often remain important stakeholders—as investors, sources of new talent, promoters/detractors, and customers. Bigger leaders strive to ensure that people are separated from the company with professionalism, grace, and respect, no matter the circumstances.

Succession Planning

The succession planning process focuses on ensuring a robust pipeline for talent and a plan for key roles across the company, including executive roles. It also typically identifies and elevates high-performing employees who have the potential to take on bigger roles in the organization. Even in organizations that have cast aside formal ratings, rankings, and performance evaluations, the needs of high-potential talent tend to differ from the general population.

Some might feel it discriminatory to separate out and mentor a group of employees for leadership. But the larger and more complex an organization is, the more central succession planning is for performance and career development. Because again, the workforce continues to age, and attrition is inevitable. Every day, ten thousand baby boomers reach the traditional retirement age of sixty-five. There is a constant outflow of employees retiring, even if you never lose anyone outside of retirement.

- *Check if there are too many commonalities among the high-potential talent pool.* Is favoritism or comfort coming into play? Is lookism happening? This burden shouldn't fall on just one leader. Leaders who hail from different demographics and backgrounds must ensure they truly have a pool of the most robust and diversified talent—not just leaders that look a certain way, went to a certain school, or are of a certain age group. Get an assortment of varied leaders involved in the assessment process. This will help mitigate the risk of bias driving your decision-making.

- *Potential is dynamic, not fixed.* Being high potential is not a lifetime label or status. I've encountered people who were designated as high potential for several years, then lose that label and think it's something they've done wrong, rather than a consequence of changes in the business or field. You need to make it clear what high potential means, even as that definition might change. Perhaps it's "You have the potential to advance your career by several levels." It might be time bound: "We see that happening in two or three years." Make sure everyone knows that you're tailoring this designation to the current needs of the business. Otherwise, people will assume bias is involved, as opposed to more tangible things like having an MBA to become an executive, having an engineering degree to run a technical team, etc.

- *Be transparent about the criteria for and status of succession planning.* Organizations often struggle with how to talk about who is high potential, and thus who isn't. So some companies keep it a secret. I disagree with this approach. Bigger leaders tell people where they stand and what they need to do to achieve their career aspirations. These conversations can feel risky if you're dealing with people who think they should be high potential but who don't have the qualifications. Being confronted with the fact that they aren't considered high potential may discourage them. On the other hand, it may motivate them to achieve new goals. For me, this happened when I was unwilling to relocate to a different place during a part of my career. It was a conscious choice for me, as I was prioritizing living close to my parents. Predictably, I "fell off" the high-potential track. I knew that this was my choice and that my decision would negatively impact my future opportunities, but that didn't fully alleviate the sting when I missed out on promotions simply because of my address. It motivated me to get engaged in other facets of the company and even amp up my involvement in philanthropic organizations to keep my motivation and engagement up. Later on, as my children grew older and career advancement became a greater priority, we were willing to move for the right opportunity. What needs to be clear to all employees is that high-potential status does not guarantee a promotion, nor is it a requirement to progress in your career. Sure, it can help, but make it clear that plenty of people who do not have this designation have thrived otherwise.

- *Remember that workers who are not high-potential still have aspirations that must be nurtured.* In your environment, some may define success as being an innovative leader, or your best individual contributors might relish a reputation and compensation as a star performer, or your long-tenured, deeply knowledgeable workers might quite enjoy their position as the group sage.

In the opening of this chapter, I mentioned that what made a successful team yesterday is not what's going to make today's team successful, nor will it fuel the success of the teams of tomorrow. Herein lies the power of diverse teams: experiential learning is one of the most effective forms of learning, and it's often done with other people. The more diverse people we engage with, the more opportunities for learning and understanding we are presented with, and the more growth we can experience, both personally and professionally.

Lead Bigger by Championing Vitality

- Does your organization currently define an employee lifecycle? After reading this chapter, do you think any elements of it should be adjusted? What new approaches or steps will you take to improve?

- What talent will you need in the next two to five years? Where is that talent—and are you there, too? What is your reputation as an employer? Does it vary depending on demographics and other dimensions, including geography, industry, sector?

- Are your leaders having distinct career conversations with their workforce? Are they comfortable discussing future aspirations beyond the employee's current role or even outside of your organization? Are people leaving you for better career opportunities? If so, why?

- How does your organization nurture top talent? Are the criteria for making those lists clear, equitable, and seen positively by the workforce? What are your metrics—qualitative and quantitative? What do the trends reveal to you?

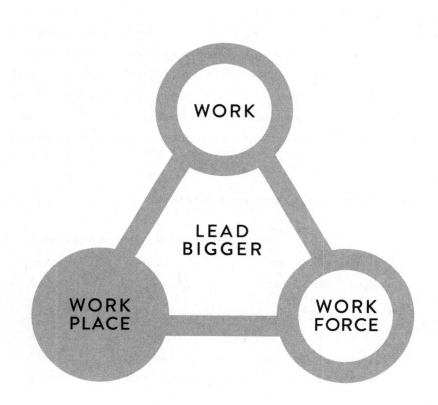

PART THREE

YOUR TRUSTED, AGILE WORKPLACE

In my framework, I use the term *workplace* to describe the overall work environment and *workspace* to describe the physical locations of work, whether they are manufacturing plants, retail stores, corporate offices, virtual offices, vehicles, or other sites. The workplace includes the many workspaces where the workforce gets their job done.

Bigger leaders create an environment for their workforce to thrive, and the foundation for thriving is **SAFETY.** In addition to physical safety, leaders must create psychologically safe work environments, even when factors outside your control are disrupting your workforce. As work has transformed over the past several years, the **BOUNDARIES** between people's personal lives and professional lives have blurred. Those boundaries are no longer the same for any two people on your team—they aren't even the same for one person on any given day. We work at different times, in different places, on tasks that sometimes can be done asynchronously and sometimes must be done synchronously with others, in person or digitally. Without bigger leadership, this workplace complexity can contribute to stress and burnout, as well as confusion and a lack of clarity on how leaders can enable productivity, engagement, and high performance.

A key skill of bigger leaders is their ability to connect the dots. Of course, they do this in their organizations and industry, but they also move with an eye toward long-term lasting impact. To illustrate this, we'll explore how a country's birth rate, known as its total fertility rate, has urgent implications for business growth and leadership.

We close this section with **FLEXIBILITY,** a winning trait of the workplace and our teams. The most successful teams will be those who are agile and resilient, because change will forever be the only constant. Bigger leaders understand that the when, where, and how of a productive workplace will vary from employee to employee, from project to project. Inclusive workplaces adapt to the unique needs of individuals in order to bring the best out of each person and out of the team as a whole. One size truly no longer fits all.

CHAPTER EIGHT

SAFETY
CREATE AN ENVIRONMENT
THAT FUELS CONTRIBUTION

Our people's expectations of a safe workplace have expanded beyond physical safety to include psychological safety. Bigger leaders set the tone and create an environment for their teams in which people feel safe and trusted. The workforce is then empowered to take smart risks, innovate, engage in constructive discourse, and be themselves—all while working together toward common goals.

Throughout the course of my career, I've had an opportunity to work with all kinds of wonderful leaders. And while it was the exception, there were also times when I experienced a challenging relationship. Such a challenge could occur if a leader's dominant style was demeaning and demoralizing, voice raised in a type of caustic intolerance, even in spitfire rage when they were dissatisfied. It's awful to be on the receiving end of it, to say the least. Huddling with colleagues, trying to figure out the manager's mood of the day was like attempting to find the answer to an unsolvable puzzle. Constantly walking on eggshells is no way to work, much less live. How could people be at their best in such a climate? I knew I couldn't, so when I found myself in those rare situations, my priority was to find a path to a different role as soon as possible.

As my career progressed, I realized that one of the most important roles I played was to serve as the protector of my people. Once when I was responsible for a large global team, I found myself in a lively, respectful debate with my boss. He and I got along quite well, but I had yet to learn about *his* boss. I was shocked when he suggested to me that if I did not comply with a certain effort that his boss would come down and rain hellfire on me and my team. Did I feel safe at that moment? Absolutely not. What I did feel, though, was an overwhelming desire to ensure that my team wouldn't be subject to such words and threats. I did my best to keep an eye out for this person, so that I could defuse any situation that might arise. I knew, deep down, that my obligation as a bigger leader was to inoculate my team so they would be less affected by the broader noxious environment.

When members of my team encountered these kinds of conflicts, I would discuss the experience with them and assure them that I had their backs. I value emotions, and I'm not suggesting that they don't have a place in the workplace. But I believe bigger leaders should be thoughtful in how they speak, keeping themselves and others in check to make sure that they're not crossing a line that might go beyond passion to making people feel fearful or unsafe. The bigger leader must also build the resilience and grit of all members of their team, because as part of any business reality, encountering difficult situations and dealing with difficult people are inevitable.

Expectations for Safety in the Workplace

Physical safety and even digital safety in the work environment are institutional expectations. If you do business with or work for a particular company, you expect that company to keep you safe. In fact, there is a comprehensive category of regulatory requirements that address environment, health, and safety (EHS) concerns, so "do no harm" is not just preached but practiced.

And with the rise of the importance of mental health and wellness, safety as a concept is expanding beyond just physical safety to encompass emotional and mental safety as well. Harvard Business School professor Amy Edmondson first coined the term *psychological safety* in 1999, which she defined as "an absence of interpersonal fear." In other words, it is the belief that employees will not be punished for surfacing ideas, questions, concerns, or mistakes.

Psychological safety is *relational,* stemming from people interacting with one another. The institution cannot fully "policy" its way to psychological safety or put controls in place to automate it. While employers have an institutional responsibility to implement protections against bullying or harassment, employee assistance hotlines, and robust mental health benefits, these measures are insufficient. Creating psychological safety in the workforce is the responsibility of leaders and how they interact with other people. Of course the organization or company can commit to safety as a core value, but the assurance of this safety is in the hands of leaders and team members.

As you might expect, in psychologically safe environments, performance goes up, along with constructive conflict and increased collaboration; negative discord goes down; and there's a higher level of risk-taking, experimentation, and innovation. As Laura Delizonna of Stanford University writes, "We become more open-minded, resilient, motivated, and persistent when we feel safe. Humor increases, as does solution-finding and divergent thinking—the cognitive process underlying creativity."

Leaders can certainly create environments in which microaggressions, bullying, and discrimination are not tolerated. But unlike physical safety, where the organization can more heavily control many factors associated with their workspaces, a person's feeling of safety can be impacted by factors outside the leader or organization's control. How so? The proliferation of hate crimes, the tragic loss of life from mass shootings, judicial actions and legislation, inflammatory words used by public figures and the media, and organizational politics are all examples. And like it or not, these issues infiltrate the workplace. When challenges arise that are outside our control but within our circle of concern, we may be deeply affected, carrying a burden that can show up in our performance. Imagine being the mother of a trans teen working on the same team as a man who was pictured in a local newspaper protesting a drag queen story hour at a local bookstore. Or the aunt of a school shooting victim working with someone with a progun bumper sticker on his car in the lot.

After the 2021 mass shooting at a spa in Atlanta, where six of the eight people killed were Asian women, I spent time with groups of my Asian employees sharing feelings of anger, frustration, and despair, while providing a shoulder for them to lean on. They observed that their colleagues were at a loss of what to say and that some people were, to their dismay, insisting that the crime was not racially motivated. I myself had heard such comments. I realized that this was an opportunity to bring people together to improve empathy and understanding. In several small group sessions, I gathered a cross section of people (Asian and non-Asian) and led a conversation about how we were processing this latest round of tragedies. There were tears, hugs, and lots of communication. My objective was to help each person see a bigger picture, considering the perspectives of colleagues different from them, and realize that these differences could actually deepen our respect for one another and improve our connection. As bigger leaders, while we may not understand *why* an external event affects someone deeply, we must respect the fact that it *does*. This conversation was sensitive, but by having it, we restored a sense of psychological safety between these colleagues, allowing them to defuse an emotionally charged situation and resume their collaboration to get work done.

Upon reflection, we had already established a sufficient degree of psychological safety to enable these people to come together and the conversation to take place. Remember it's a gift if a group or individual allows you in to support them, to better understand their struggle. And if they allow us, we must seek to empathize with them so we can more effectively support them.

Safety Myths

Certain advice about psychological safety is actually problematic. One misapprehension is that the end goal is to be fearless. But when you look at what's happening in the world, how can you stop fear from happening? Volatility, uncertainty, complexity, and change are constant and will permeate your work environment no matter what you do. The word *fearless* misleads people, to the point that they might ask themselves, *What's wrong with me? Maybe I'm not cut out to be a leader because leaders are supposed to be indomitable.* It can lead to unhealthy impostor syndrome and may trigger people to question whether they deserve or are qualified to be in leadership positions.

I don't believe we'll ever operate in the complete absence of fear. It's part of life and serves the healthy and necessary human purpose of gauging risk. Just as to be human is to have bias, to be human is to experience fear.

Instead, we should focus on developing trust and resilience so we can handle the difficulties that come our way. Courage is not a lack of fear; it's the ability to move ahead in the face of fear. Some of the hallmarks of a safe environment are people feeling comfortable in sharing their thoughts, bringing up their concerns and disagreements while constructively working through them with others. We want to respectfully acknowledge that we all have different levels of comfort with risk and that the leader is there to support each member of the team. Leading bigger means bringing fear out in the open, which requires vulnerability about our state of being. A difficult task, but it's the catalyst to getting unstuck, to putting things in perspective, and to helping you regain control of yourself. When we help others around us focus their attention ahead, individual and team performance improve. Yet DDI's Global Leadership Forecast found that only 24 percent of senior leadership are comfortable showing vulnerability at work.

A second myth is that psychological safety and mental well-being are soft priorities, less important than your quantitative objectives. Part of the false narrative today is that tending to psychological safety means we are moonlighting as therapists, creating safe spaces instead of facing reality. According to this myth, we're not allowed to reprimand somebody or to give feedback; instead, we must be nice about everything. Granted, we do have an obligation to be professional, civil, and respectful, which is not the same as being nice all the time. Tough feedback and decisions can be delivered kindly with conviction and facts. There will always be hard decisions to be made, including layoffs, and these can always be done humanely. But make no mistake about it: a sense of psychological safety is a direct driver of performance. According to McKinsey, "In extensive research ranging from medical teams in hospitals to software development teams at Big Tech firms, psychological safety is consistently one of the strongest predictors of team performance, productivity, quality, safety, creativity, and innovation."

Which brings me to a third myth: that the goal of psychological safety is to create the feeling that employees are all part of a "work family." This language goes against every pillar of a psychologically safe work environment. The individuals you work with are not your family (unless of course you're in your own family-run business!), and the more you use such language, the more inappropriate expectations your people might have about boundaries and accountability, including lifelong tenure. The reality is, employees can be laid off for poor performance or let go in mass layoffs, which is not something that happens in families, and in such situations workers who think of themselves as part of a "work family" will feel betrayed, their trust broken, their psychological safety taking a hit.

A word I like to use instead is *camaraderie*. We all want camaraderie and colleagues we trust, and we want to have some fun with our people. Camaraderie offers us real engagement with one another, a connection greater than just acquaintances or work colleagues. It helps build comfort and trust, which contribute to strong feelings of psychological safety. If you could be a fly on the wall at one of my staff meetings, you might be concerned at the sarcasm, playful jabs, and laughs involved. But if you stayed around for a couple of weeks, you would realize that we trusted and respected one another and were in tight alignment to achieve our common goals. Bottom line, we felt safe with one another (a sentiment similar to how my customer service team and I felt as they presented me with the yellow mug that I mentioned at the beginning of this book!).

Creating Psychological Safety for Your Team

Think back to the discussion of the importance of aligning corporate values with actual leadership behaviors in chapter 3. Many organizations have values associated with safety, including the expectation that they'll support people speaking up: *Just do the right thing. See something, say something.* But these sayings are just platitudes if you don't have a culture that backs them up. Bigger leaders help create this trusted, safe environment by being open and vulnerable themselves, demonstrating care and compassion while ensuring that there are clear boundaries and that actions are taken when these are crossed.

So how does the bigger leader implement this?

Look inward. Bigger leaders start with themselves, thinking through their own behavior. The most powerful lever in creating psychologically safe interactions is your own behavior. People look to their leaders for cues on language, decisions, and interpersonal relationships, and they notice the type of people leaders surround themselves with. In many ways, when you sign up to be a leader, you agree to serve as a model for others. That just comes with the territory. You need to be open about your mistakes, concerns, and fears to demonstrate that we all struggle at times.

Oftentimes, especially when you have a geographically diverse, even global team, what is acceptable in one culture may not be appropriate in another. The appropriateness of bows, handshakes, hugs, and even kisses on the cheek in business settings varies. Pointing your finger is considered rude in some cultures, as is using your left hand to point or eat. Forgo a long lunch in some locations, and your colleagues will wonder if you are avoiding them.

While these may seem like minor things, as a bigger leader, if you are to demonstrate respect for and build trust with all your workers, you must learn these nuances and demonstrate them. Of course you can't know all the nuances of what constitutes psychological safety for every member or group on your team. So what do you do? If you're uncertain, respectfully ask. And carefully observe the reaction of those around you. Ask for and get feedback. The creation of a psychologically safe workplace is not a one-and-done thing. You must continue to evolve and cultivate it, especially as your team composition changes.

Make it safe to discuss failures. In the sales profession, teams are loath to talk about customers they've lost. Having spent half my career in B2B sales, responsible for revenue growth, I have many years of firsthand experience with this phenomenon. With every new role I've had in sales, the first ninety days were filled with my teams testing my leadership. They wanted to know if I was one of those command-and-control leaders who would find losses intolerable and immediately assign blame. In fact, one of the tongue-in-cheek comments you'll often get from salespeople is that they lost a deal because of price, but they won a deal because of their relationship with the customer! Fortunately, having been on the front lines myself, I knew how psychologically difficult (and often thrilling) sales could be. After all, salespeople need to sustain optimism despite constant rejection. Perhaps this is why my approach to sales meetings in which we reviewed wins and losses was to make it okay to talk about anything, to be vulnerable in sharing mistakes, not to engage in public lambastings if things didn't always work out as planned. And importantly to perpetually embrace learning as a necessary outcome. We would highlight both wins and losses with our teams so we could get better together.

I've always believed that there are only two possible outcomes—success and/or learning. Good days and growth days. Failure is a necessary part of the growth process. You can use any alleged failure to develop a growth mindset. Of course feeling the sting of failure is absolutely normal. When I was rejected in my early attempts to secure a role in sales, my first reaction was that I'd failed. In reality, each rejection constituted a chance for introspection, learning, and action on my part, so those low moments helped me spring higher later on. According to researchers, employees with a growth mindset are more likely to foster innovation, because they "are more apt to try new strategies to attain goals and to learn from mistakes and others' strengths."

Give feedback with a future focus; don't get stuck in the past. As a leader, you need to be direct and candid, and when you give feedback, make sure it's always done in a way that's forward looking. Sometimes we spend too much time trying to psychoanalyze or explain a certain behavior when it's impossible to replicate the situation anyway. Of course you want to understand what happened, but it's more important to discuss how you might handle it differently when a similar situation arises.

Psychologically Unsafe Environments: The Toxic Workplace

What is the opposite of a psychologically safe environment? That would be an unsafe workplace, also categorized as toxic. Such workplaces and bosses are poisonous but frighteningly common, to the point where almost half of American workers wouldn't wish their job on their worst enemy.

Toxic environments lack boundaries between personal and professional priorities, as well as boundaries around time and role, due to a lack of clarity and oftentimes a lack of caring. Disrespect, an intolerance for mistakes (unless made by someone in the in-crowd), and unhealthy relationships plague these workplaces. This is where command-and-control leaders, who lead through hierarchy, coercive power, intimidation, and permission-based actions, have the upper hand; it's their way or the highway. And when people exhibit bad behavior in such environments, they are not held accountable for it. "Us versus them" language within the same company is a big marker. Lack of diverse representation in leadership is another sign of a possibly toxic environment, one filled with bias. Backstabbing, saying one thing but doing another, belittling others to elevate oneself, valuing confidence over competence, and behaving like a chameleon to ensure one's own survival are common. Bad politics, disingenuousness, and manipulation abound.

Toxic work cultures are filled with finger-pointing leaders. Ironically these leaders are often filled with unbounded ego and overbearing confidence. There's also gaslighting, defined as attempting to make someone believe that they are going insane, a form of misleading others for one's own advantage; gaslighting is now so common that it was Merriam-Webster's word of the year in 2022. Often a toxic environment will have a front of disingenuous positivity; everyone is expected to be over-the-top rah-rah, which masks the problems underneath (and prevents anyone from calling them out). If you feel that your self-esteem is being chipped away and that your mental health is suffering, these are likely signs you're in a toxic environment.

To suss out toxicity, pay attention to situations in which people are quiet and their energy seems suppressed. This applies to customers, team members, and anyone whom you care about engaging with. When I was in sales, I encouraged my teams to view all feedback from customers as worthy, even if it was emotional or extremely negative. Because if clients still cared enough to express themselves, you had a chance to turn that relationship around. Customer silence is a giant red flag because it indicates that customers are shopping somewhere else, they don't care enough to speak up, they believe their voice doesn't matter, or they don't trust you. The same is true of the workforce. When people are silent—whether it's in town hall meetings, in group sessions, or in a project team—it's often a symptom that they are intimidated or apprehensive. Post-pandemic, a new term was coined, *quiet quitting,* which can be an earmark of a toxic culture. This is not just a phenomenon of Western culture. In China, such behavior is called *lying flat* (a phrase that translates loosely to the American idiom "lying down on the job"), and it came about as a reaction to the pressures of overworking. This developed into an informal social movement characterized by intentional low motivation, low drive, and indifference.

Contrary to what some people think, a toxic workplace is not about hating the what of your job, although if you do, that will certainly make work less fulfilling. It's more about the how and who that impact you at work. Having had seventeen different jobs and twenty-six different bosses in my corporate career, I've worked in a wide range of environments over the years. Through my own experiences, including as a coach and mentor to leaders across industries, I'll share two of the most common characteristics of toxic environments, poor leadership and a lack of growth investment.

Poor leadership includes bad bosses who embody small leadership behaviors such as blaming and micromanaging. They lack integrity and often don't respect others. It's evident in how they treat their workers—except for their favorites, of course. Toxic bosses can be bullies or narcissists, and some are woefully insecure. Bosses who are doormats are no better, seemingly adding absolutely no value to the work or the team. Such leaders are unable to establish a common purpose and make tough decisions—which, of course, makes it harder for you to get your job done well.

A second characteristic of toxic environments is a distinct lack of growth investment. Contrary to popular belief, HR is not responsible for training and development—leaders are, both for themselves and for their people. If an organization doesn't invest in continuous learning, then the bottom line is that they lack commitment to their growth. This type of toxicity can be more subtle. While there may be plenty of focus on the job and improvements in productivity, very little attention is paid to the development of new skills in employees or to their career paths. We all want to realize our fullest potential, whatever that means for each of us. Providing options based on people's needs and aspirations is part of your obligation as the bigger leader. If you happen to work in an environment where this does not exist, you must create it—through partnerships with HR or external experts including schools, educational programs, and otherwise. You must create a safe environment where people can express their interests, help to shape their learning plans, and make resources available to them that help them grow in their current and future roles.

The bigger leader focuses on both their people's performance development *and* their career development.

If you have to watch your back, CYA, and reread your emails ten times before sending them, all while being aware that your company doesn't care about your growth, you will likely find it impossible to get anything done. A toxic environment is like buckets of sand being thrown into the gears of your business. High-trust environments create a well-oiled flywheel.

How to Lead Bigger in a Toxic Environment

As an individual, what do you do when you're in a toxic environment and/or work for a toxic boss? I've found a multipronged approach helpful. This guidance applies to anyone, whether you formally consider yourself a leader or not. Think of these points as elements of a survival strategy. First, document key points and interactions, including your accomplishments, at least monthly. Second, use this data to work your relationship with key leaders. Figure out what "leading small" attributes you're dealing with, and tailor your approach to them, working to get them on your side. Seek counsel from trusted colleagues who have direct experience in what works and what doesn't, and shape your own plan that you can authentically deliver. Third—which may sound seemingly impossible—is diversifying your support base far beyond your boss. I have always found HR a tremendous ally throughout my career. I have also benefited from the support of executive sponsors who knew my performance, character, and potential. Lean on them and cultivate connections not only inside of your organization but outside; include customers, partners, and others who benefit from your work. But be careful; there are times when HR professionals are co-opted by small leaders. Whatever the case, do try to dilute the leadership toxicity around you. Fourth, do not emulate those bad behaviors! Be the bigger leader and you'll find that you become a magnet for people who want real leadership.

The previous tips were focused on you as an individual, to ensure you can survive. Next, consider your role as a leader of people, thinking about how you can improve the culture. If you're leading in a pervasively toxic environment, you have some important decisions to make. Most critically, since you're the leader of a team, you may find yourself more deeply affected when things don't go well. You need to assess the risk to yourself and your own safety, especially if you are the primary breadwinner for dependents and loved ones. Understand that some of your people are likely going through this, too. Constant worry about your situation can also cause problems with your physical health. Ask yourself: If the environment is damaging to your mental health, is the cost worth it? Can you try to change the environment? Should you? What power do you have to implement change? What role do you have in attempting to improve this toxic environment? If you can't muster the conviction you can help, it will be unrealistic to expect your teams to. And don't forget, the level of risk to your reputation you take on will be greater than if you were just a member of the team, because your scope of responsibilities is greater and the entire team is watching carefully how you respond.

Next, if you do plan to stick it out, you must shield your team. Passing down the stress to them will only undercut their ability to perform and increase your odds of failure. They need to stay focused on the task at hand. But to remain credible, you also want to demonstrate to them that you are aware of what the reality is. Make it clear that you will continue to represent them and push for the best outcomes. Being naively optimistic doesn't help. Identify the root cause by speaking to employees who are witnessing the conflict.

If you choose to confront the person who is the source of the toxicity in hopes of making things better, give them the benefit of the doubt in the conversation. Don't assume that their behaviors are consciously chosen to negatively impact others.

Schedule a meeting with them. Here's a possible approach to set the context for the conversation: "*Name*, I appreciate you taking the time to meet with me. I'd like to talk to you about our team and this critical work that we're doing together." If they are senior to you and in a position of power, it's good to lean into this: "My team and I value your leadership and your perspectives. We know we couldn't get this done without you." Then get their perspective early in the conversation to spot any biases and concerns they may have. What you're looking for is insight into the why of their toxic behavior. "What are your thoughts on how things are going? Are there areas you'd like us to do better? Are we meeting your needs thus far—in terms of communications and milestones?" Use a positive but pragmatic tone. Unpack what the toxic person is saying, separate it from negative or emotional rhetoric, and uncover their truth. Resist the temptation to get caught up in bad-mouthing or gossiping. Be sure you're clear about what could be better, but do not make it personal. "You know, our team would really benefit from some ad hoc recognition, especially given all the long hours they've been working," or "I know the team would find great insight into your perspective about corporate strategy and our direction to help reinforce how critical our role is. Would you be willing to spend some time with the team?" Bigger leaders don't succumb to the "us vs. them" mentality.

The human source of toxicity may need to be convinced of your team's strategy and output. You may need to expose your team to this person because it's necessary to get the job done. Mindfully facilitate those discussions and strive to keep them constructive. You cannot challenge a powerful, toxic person in any way that's combative, particularly in public.

You may find you need to check in more often with your team, individually and collectively, to see how they are faring and help you insulate them against some of the stress. But don't forget that you will need to lessen your stress. You need support from truly trusted confidants, which in most cases are not people within your workplace. This is a mistake that many, many people make: They aren't intentional about how (and with whom) they blow off steam. Too often, the people they've chosen to release pressure with aren't their friends but are simply coworkers. True confidants are few and far between, so be cautious when finding one person who will listen to you, to help share the burden you're carrying.

Occasionally in a difficult environment folks on your team might be suffering greatly for personal or professional reasons, but might need to hang on to the job for the moment. You might be able to help them find a fully acceptable strategy to fly beneath the radar, for the time being. For example, someone might need to focus on caring for a sick family member, so they can't commit to certain projects because of the additional time commitments involved. Another person might be feeling the warning signs of burnout and might need to temporarily slow the pace to recover. Flying under the radar is not a bad short-term strategy if done intentionally. Another all-too-common scenario in the workplace is an individual who has had a troubled history with a prior manager or coworker who has since put that individual in a perpetual "penalty box." In this case, it's sometimes better to help this person stay in the background on a project. In this situation, your objective for a period of time is to continue to contribute, but to avoid standing out, which lessens risk and your exposure to toxicity. Some tactics include shifting more communications to email and other digital forms (instead of live and in person), shifting more of your time to virtual work instead of at the office, and leveraging trusted relationships to help you surface bad news or challenging topics. The bigger leader is more than willing to do this for their people and understands that safety is also situational. Too often, I've encountered people who are really struggling because of pressures outside of the workplace, which then makes them really vulnerable at work. Inclusive leadership is about helping your people to thrive, which at times means enabling them just to tread water at work.

But ideally, if you're in a toxic culture for a sustained period, you'll want to change your situation. I've often said that you never want to leave a job because of one person, but I understand that if that one person creating the toxicity is someone like your boss, the situation can be extremely difficult. Depending on your environment, you can assess whether bosses change very frequently and balance the risk accordingly: Will the situation resolve itself over time? Can you find enough safety and support until then? Where the line is drawn is entirely subjective, but you have to consciously think about where to draw it for yourself. The objective of your life is to not fly under the radar; it's to be the best you can be and realize your fullest potential, sharing whatever greatness is in you to make a difference.

Final Notes

The original definition of psychological safety—an absence of interpersonal fear that allows employees to raise work-related issues—was narrower than what it has now become, to the point where some leaders are concerned about becoming pseudo-therapists to their workforce. What we've discussed clarifies the expectations of what leaders need to take on. Remember Professor Edmondson's definition that psychological safety entails feeling safe to bring up concerns about *work-related content.* Ultimately, the role of the inclusive leader is one of professional purpose. While modern leadership requires embracing larger aspects of well-being, the boundaries must remain clear. Dynamically setting those boundaries well is a distinct behavior of bigger leaders. We'll discuss this in the next chapter.

Lead Bigger by Ensuring Safety

- How does your organization currently define safety? Which leaders or departments are in charge of it? Should that responsibility be modified?

- Reflect on an experience when you felt psychologically safe on a team. Now think of a time you worked in a more toxic environment. What happened to your results in both cases? What was the leader's role in influencing or creating those environments? What elements of both experiences show up on your current team?

- Since organizations cannot "policy" their way to psychological safety, how can you increase it on your team(s)? How do you plan to address safety individually and collectively?

CHAPTER NINE

BOUNDARIES

NAVIGATE PROFESSIONAL AND PERSONAL REALITIES

Work is what we do, not a place we go to. Each employee establishes their own boundaries between work and home. Bigger leaders recognize that those boundaries vary in rigidity by person and over time. These leaders cultivate different modalities to achieve high performance no matter where people are.

I have countless childhood memories of my dad going to work and my mom staying at home. There was always a clear delineation of labor and role. My father was the traditional breadwinner and my mom ran the household, which included taking the lead on childcare. Our special family trips into my dad's office shaped my adolescent view that going to work was an exciting thing, something to which I aspired.

One of the most notable characterizations of work, which was accentuated if there was only one parent or caregiver, was the fact that to work meant one had to leave the home. In between was a commute. Even as I entered the workforce, the border between personal and professional was clearly drawn. The boundaries that separated work from home were physical and logistical, which also enforced mental and emotional boundaries.

Let's take a brief look back in history. At one point, the farm *was* life for the whole family. The separation between work and home happened only after the industrial revolution, when work moved to the factory and office. Domestic and professional roles diverged and gender roles were set. Whether it was at the factory or in an office, work was a place we went to, and home was our sanctuary away from work.

As our world grew more technologically advanced, we could increasingly be quite productive almost anywhere at any time. Of course, many roles are still wedded to specific locations, but today, work is no longer a place that we go to, it's something we do. As such, our workplace has become increasingly fluid. Boundaries have become less meaningful in this context, as we consider what we must get done and how and when we must do it.

While many employees have a clear sense of what is private and what is a part of their work life, sometimes the leaders themselves need to put guardrails in place so that the lines are not blurred. For instance, employee assistance programs can be critical for workers who have

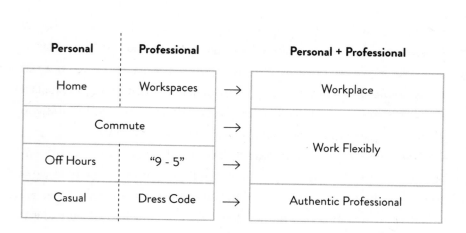

	Then			Now
Personal	**Professional**		**Personal + Professional**	
Home	Workspaces	→	Workplace	
Commute		→	Work Flexibly	
Off Hours	"9 - 5"	→		
Casual	Dress Code	→	Authentic Professional	

personal struggles that are having an effect on their work: for example, a worker who is struggling with alcoholism. These programs allow the employee to access help privately, as a healthcare issue, protected by health privacy laws.

Yet more often it's the companies themselves that tend to overstep logical boundaries. As the dust settled from the disruptions of the pandemic, we've seen companies trying to reinstate old techniques for policing their employees, often with very low-trust methods, such as software that monitors productivity, badge swipes, and "bed checks," where managers walk floors to see if people are at their desks. The lack of trust is evident. Employees feel as though they are being treated like children. This hurts any sense of empowerment, well-being, and pride.

As a reminder, we're defining *workspace* as the physical location where you are actually working, whether it's at home, on the road, in the air, in the office, or wherever. And we're using the term *workplace* as descriptive of the entire work environment, which is where the policies and practices and power and politics are relevant across any given organization, team, or business. Bigger leaders maintain boundaries when we don't have the separation of physical space or clarity of time to help us draw them. Yes, this can be a double-edged sword, and as leaders, we must become cognizant of the nuances if we are to serve and support our teams most effectively.

Maintaining Boundaries to Support Well-Being

Traditional managers question workers' commitment if they're not reachable at certain times or are unwilling to stay late at management's beck and call. These expectations can be levied on the employee like a career tax. I've encountered countless people who expect you to burn the midnight oil and allow work emergencies to interrupt family/personal time; sometimes it's unintentional, but other times it's just considered par for the course. In speaking with numerous Gen Zers who are now in the active workforce, I've learned that the when and where of the work is just as relevant as the why and the what.

Some employees want to immerse themselves in their jobs because it's integral to their career and identity (and data on belonging tells us this is more likely to be senior executives). Others want an arm's length between them and their job because their job is, well, a job. Time is a precious resource, and it's one of the most often violated boundaries.

While my generation has been trained to blend work life and home life as a necessary evil, up-and-coming generations will not. Although certain fervent multitaskers prefer to work that way, it cannot be an expectation of the future workplace. Either way, how many hours you work or how fast you respond to an email shouldn't be the barometer of productivity and performance. Nor should a rigid take on where you work determine your potential. Bigger leaders must ask themselves if the ways they've been measuring success and individual effectiveness are truly relevant today.

Authenticity

After surveying 1,500 members of Gen Z, Ernst & Young reported: "Authenticity is the most important value for Gen Z—even beyond future plans and being rich. . . . The vast majority of Gen Z respondents reported that authenticity is more important than any other personal value tested, including spending time on things that will help their futures, independence, changing the world, and being rich or famous."

I've come to define authenticity as knowing who you are (including who you're aspiring to be) and staying true to it. Your authenticity is captured in what you do and how you do it, with full understanding of your why. Your beliefs, thoughts, behaviors, and actions are aligned, and this shines through in your character, spirit, and personality. Throughout my career, I've coined a hashtag intended to encourage others to embrace their authenticity: #BeRealBeTrueBeYOU. This aspiration isn't just for the younger workers. To a degree, we've all gotten used to the integration of our personal and professional personas. In fact, Merriam-Webster's word of the year for 2023 was *authentic*.

Perhaps you resonate deeply with this idea, or maybe you're rolling your eyes at such an overly hyped concept. The reality is that authenticity has become more relevant and a requirement for leading bigger. According to BetterUp, the powerful benefits to showing up authentically in the workplace include:

- 140 percent increase in employee engagement
- 50 percent increase in team performance
- 90 percent increase in team innovation
- 54 percent lower turnover
- 150 percent increase in belonging

Clearly, authenticity is good for the individual, the team, and the organization as a whole.

Safety tip: Bringing your whole self to work doesn't mean you should *show* your whole self at work. Understanding what boundaries to establish is an art, not a science, and your choice in how much you want to reveal often varies by situation. Consider establishing boundaries in these areas:

- Your life story, personal history, and personal life details.
- Delineating relationships—for example, not all colleagues will become friends and not all friends are confidants.
- Opinions, ideologies, beliefs, political views, sense of humor.

I've already shared that I grew up in New Jersey and raised my family there for several decades, proudly characterizing myself as a Jersey Girl.

Among many things, this means I speak quickly. I gravitate toward a direct and pragmatic style, and I sprinkle Jersey-isms into my casual speech (such as "you guys," "are you kidding me?!" and "it's all good"). When I moved to a different part of the country, it became clear to me that the genuine me, stylistically, was not as effective. I was having a harder time getting my points across and creating connections. I learned that softening my approach, speaking more slowly, and minimizing the use of my Jersey slang were helpful—and enabled others to hear me better. Part of leading bigger is making adjustments that need to be made to better the overall outcome. The changes I made didn't mean that I wasn't being myself; they just meant I wasn't showing that part of me in certain situations because it had an impact on my efficacy, including my ability to build meaningful relationships through communication.

We know that with our people, their whole self is part of our team, and our job is to ensure they see the greatness within them. Bigger leaders help their people see their greatness, believe in it, and unleash it. And part of this unleashing is the refinement of the art of bringing (as opposed to showing) our authenticity at work and in other settings.

Gathering with Intention

In the past, some employees made a career out of face time. The idea was that the more face time you had with leaders, the better off you'd be. Think back to people around you throughout your career who were the beneficiaries of proximity bias (the tendency to prefer people who are physically closer at hand). And likely each of us has encountered situations where face time was not just the means but the goal itself. How else could leaders gauge your leadership style, your executive presence, your commitment, and your potential?

But only a tenth of employees now consider face time with management a valid reason to go into a physical office. They are willing to head back to the office if the time is spent on collaboration or camaraderie.

There are absolute benefits to bringing people together. Sometimes nothing but gathering around the good old-fashioned whiteboard for coming up with ideas will do.

You can't replace the in-person dynamic of building relationships, experiencing culture, learning body language and other nonverbal cues, and enjoying in-person mentorship. Leaders need to be thoughtful about their intention when they bring people into the office or ask them to gather somewhere. I'm a huge advocate for annual kickoffs, leadership summits, time spent in the market (with customers, employees, and partners), and unique in-person learning experiences. You bring people together, rally around a vision and strategy, meet the faces behind the names, spend both structured and unstructured time together, have some fun, and form deep relationships. It does wonders to establish culture and set a foundation of trust between people, with a focus on growth.

Beyond gathering for annual or quarterly events, you can effectively reimagine your workplace, starting with the understanding that your workplace includes a vast array of workspaces. These workspaces include traditional company office buildings and other function-driven sites such as manufacturing or R&D locations, distribution centers and warehouses, field sales and service centers, and so on. But now bigger leaders must stretch their thinking to embrace flexible workspaces such as remote home offices, fleets, and locations on customer premises. We now must think of the corporate office space in the same way as those spaces: driven by need, used to enhance both short-term and long-term performance while fostering cultures of growth and belonging. Rather than return-to-the-office (RTO) mandates that focus on the actual presence of employees and the assumption of improved productivity, leaders should structure their workspaces for collaboration, for culture, for innovation, and for the accomplishment of objectives best implemented in person.

Start with why you need people in these workspaces. Coming up with reasons physical proximity is better can help leaders explain when physical co-location is needed. Consider some of these leadership priorities that could benefit from intentional in-person gatherings:

- Building trust-based relationships

- Creating belonging and purpose

- Demonstrating allyship and support

- Enhancing creativity and collaboration

- Getting to know each other better

- Blue-sky thinking and brainstorming for innovation

- Celebrating key milestones and successes

- Connecting for coaching, mentorship, and sponsorship

- Sharing in unique learning experiences with real-time engagement

- Delivering meaningful feedback

But these things will not magically manifest themselves simply because people are together in a workspace. We've all heard stories of colleagues who have been summoned back to the office only to sit at a desk and work alone. Bigger leaders must create new tactics and plans with their managers to structure opportunities to collaborate, communicate, and grow connections, while feeding a healthy culture. Treat workspaces as a vital tool in your leadership tool kit that must be employed purposefully.

Your workspaces must be an asset to your workforce and add to your culture instead of contradicting or detracting from it. Some key considerations:

- Make sure there's enough space for those who need it, when they need it.

- Shared collaboration spaces should accommodate changing needs and be optimized for teaming sessions and activities.

- Having the right tech is a must: frictionless reservation systems, capacity management tools, utilization metrics, and feedback mechanisms.

- Make the spaces inspirational, comfortable, and energizing. Don't skimp. Proper ergonomics, use of brand colors and values, digital signage, and even amenities such as coffee and snacks can help people feel good about the space they're in, boosting their connection to you.

- Don't forget about the conveniences, and especially inclusive ones. For instance, do you really want your star manager to have to run down to a different floor because they unexpectedly need a feminine hygiene product before they can launch that big brainstorming session that starts in seven minutes? Ask a diverse array of employees if they feel they belong in the space.

- Your spaces should pass the test of employee pride. Would you be willing to host your customers and your family there? Your workspaces should reflect your core and aspirational values. Consider these spaces an asset for recruiting top talent.

- Offer stipends to employees to meet their hybrid needs. No matter the location or workspace, having the right tech equipment and applications to optimally do their job is a must.

And don't forget, as a leader, you will likely have some people who may never enter a company-owned workspace. So they may not be able to benefit from the culture-enveloping environment that other colleagues will. I've seen this dynamic poorly managed by many companies—the gap between what workers based in the corporate headquarters experience and what everyone else does grows the farther away from the sun you are, with virtual workers experiencing the least connection to the organization. The inclusive leader ensures that workspace strategies don't reinforce a culture of haves and have-nots.

An example of a tactic I've used to deal with the new ways of work is structuring my leadership summits to include a hybrid approach for attendees. Some would join in person, but a larger number would join live streamed. Of course, this wasn't for the entire multiday agenda, but rather for the transparent discussions we had together. I was also sure to take care of my remote participants, giving them special swag such as snacks and gift cards for lunch to be sure they felt included in the experience. Over several years, I used the hybrid option (which amped up engagement in a big way) to expand the number of participants. The feedback I received about this bigger approach was tremendously positive, and I have no doubt that it helped us build a stronger culture of belonging, which enabled us to deliver greater performance because of enhanced trust and better alignment.

To lead inclusively across workspaces, leaders must consciously create that sense of belonging for each employee, whether they ever set foot in an official office space or not. Some areas to consider:

- Delivering an impressive and immersive onboarding process.

- Ensuring that the brand comes alive and stays alive throughout the employee's entire tenure with the organization.

- Connecting to the company's purpose and impact in tangible terms.

- Making sure that product samples or other trinkets distributed in your offices go to remote workers as well.

- Providing a budget or a consultation for ergonomic workstations at home.

- Providing parallel virtual experiences for in-person events (well-being oriented, recognition and celebration, learning).

- Adding extra personal touches with actual people to amplify the human connection. (In the areas of coaching and mentorship, this extra touch, especially one-on-one, can make a huge difference.)

- Proactively asking for feedback in fun, engaging ways like conducting live polls during gatherings or rewarding ideas for improvement with contests and prizes. When feedback is given, be sure to close the loop and share what changes have been made as a result, and what changes haven't—and why. This helps create permeability in the all-too-familiar boundary of hierarchy.

Just bringing employees into the office won't inherently create commitment and loyalty in today's environment (did it ever?). The nature of work has fundamentally shifted. People are no longer buying the traditional value proposition. As a result, 80 percent of leaders say they regret how they've handled sweeping return-to-office mandates and they would have acted differently if they'd better understood their employees.

You, as a leader, will need a new open-mindedness around the different modalities of work for your employees. Consider what work needs to be done synchronously (meaning together in real time) as opposed to what work can be done asynchronously at any time. Answer this, and right away you have found where you can inclusively create more flexibility and leave it up to the individual or the team, instead of having a more directive, prescriptive approach.

What once was rigid and fixed is now individual and ever changing: when and where we work, how much we reveal of our authentic selves, and how we connect and gather. Untethered from physical location or time zone, we each determine our boundaries as we collaborate with others. Bigger leaders model this new skill, respect each person's right to draw their own boundaries, and stay nimble as they evolve over time.

Lead Bigger Intentionally with Boundaries

- When you began your career, what were the prevailing ideas around work-life balance or the boundaries between personal and professional lives? How have those ideas changed?

- Is there any dissonance between how your current and future employees are defining their boundaries and how you define them?

- How comfortable are you with encouraging authenticity in your workforce? How could you communicate the idea of authenticity with boundaries in your culture?

- How can you structure your co-located workspaces to encourage collaboration and culture? How can you enhance your employees' private workspaces?

- How might proximity bias be affecting your workforce? Is your approach to who works where prescriptive or largely determined by the individual employee? How is that approach working for you? How is it working for your employees?

EXPLORING TOTAL FERTILITY RATE
IMPLICATIONS FOR LEADERSHIP

M ost businesspeople keep an eye on all kinds of macroeconomic indicators, such as GDP growth, unemployment, the stock market's day-to-day moves, home prices, and other indices. But hardly any give a second thought to the total fertility rate.

Yet the birth rate is a singularly important signal.

Not only is the total fertility rate a predictor of future growth in the coming years and decades, but it also tells us something about how optimistic or pessimistic our population of childbearing age feels about the future. Is there enough optimism about what the world will look like in fifty years to want to bring a child into it? Importantly, it's also a barometer of how much would-be parents are struggling today, and whether they believe they have the financial strength and enough flexibility to start a family.

This is where it's interesting to consider a natural experiment that took place over the years of the pandemic.

In 2020, the U.S. birth rate increased for the first time in seven years, causing a baby bump. Why? Economists believe that the pandemic, contrary to expectations, led to greater birth rates largely due to flexible work. Economists in the National Bureau of Economic Research wrote:

Fertility gains were concentrated in groups such as college-educated women who saw drastic reductions in the opportunity cost of having a child, when they were able to work from home and work schedules became more flexible. . . . This episode points to the large time costs of childbearing as an additional important driver of falling fertility rates and suggests that measures to alleviate these costs, such as improving child care and allowing parents more flexibility to work from home, might be associated with higher future fertility.

If flexible workplaces drove the birth rate, this suggests that businesses have an even more pivotal role to play in terms of our economic future.

How? It's widely established that a total fertility rate (TFR) of 2.1 children ensures a stable population. TFR, also known as the replacement rate, is the most important factor in population growth. When the birth rate drops, especially in the absence of immigration, the population—and thus the labor pool—ages rapidly. Why is this a problem? It impacts the total dependency ratio, the number of people in age groups not typically in the labor market—ages zero to fourteen, and older than sixty-five—compared to the number in all other age groups, multiplied by one hundred.

Over time, the decline of this ratio is a red flag for economic stability and growth, as well as the ability of the working population to support the needs (social, healthcare, financial) of the dependent population. Just before the pandemic, the TFR in the United States dropped to a record low, from 2.12 in 2007 to 1.64 in 2020, far below the healthy TFR of 2.1.

What happens to the labor pool when you drop below that rate, especially when immigration also slows? Your working population (defined as people between the ages of fifteen and sixty-four) will shrink, resulting in a talent shortage, particularly in key skill areas. Also, with an aging population that in aggregate is not being replenished, the number of people aging out of the workforce will grow. Thus those in the working population will be even more pressured to be caregivers, not only to minors but also to elders. The number of people in the labor market is outweighed by the number of those who are not, and you run the risk of a talent shortage by sheer numbers coupled with increased caregiver

Historical Total Fertility Rates for the United States

Source: SSA, The Long-Range Demographic Assumptions for the 2023 Trustees Report. (2023)

pressures on the working population. As reported in *Vox*, "In 2010, for example, there were more than seven family members available to care for each person over the age of 80; by 2030, there will be only four."

If you're a leader today and you've been unaware of the 2.1 reproductive rate, you may be caught by surprise about what's headed our way. Countries like Spain, Japan, and South Korea that have fallen below the replacement rate are already facing labor crises, and their economies are negatively impacted as a result. As Gearoid Reidy reports on Bloomberg.com, "The fertility crisis started in Japan, but it won't stay there. A declining population and plummeting fertility rate aren't unique Japanese phenomena. All rich countries will contend with this crisis." Rarely if ever is the fertility rate discussed in a leadership context; it is most often approached as a gender-equity issue, which it is—in part. But if you take a step back, it's about the good of society over the long term.

Regardless of what is happening in the political arena, companies must ensure that having and caring for children is, if not comfortable (hey, toddlers are hard!), at least within reach. After all, the birth rate is vital to the economic health of any community, country, and economy, not to mention your organization.

Yes, your organization. Alison Gemmill, a professor of population, family, and reproductive health at Johns Hopkins, told *Vox,* "We need to invest in people and their success. . . . We always hear that it takes a village, but that village is just not what it used to be. It just seems like everything's set up to be very hostile to parents."

If your company's culture is inhospitable to those who are having children, you'll find it more difficult to recruit parents, or even those who want to be parents someday—in other words, the majority of younger workers. Or if they do join, it will be with an eye on the door, knowing they will exit stage left when they do decide to have kids.

I have been known to say that true equality will not be achieved until everyone can give birth to babies. While in my younger days, I said this to demonstrate the obvious differences between the burdens on men and women. Now, after decades in corporate America, I and other leaders feel it is incumbent upon us to promote equity in the workplace through purposeful and practical means.

To be clear, *equity* does not mean everyone gets the same thing. It means being fair. And as I tell my kids all the time, *fair is not equal.* For instance, I consider it unfair to create an outsize penalty for an employee whose needs change throughout the course of their lives. If a top performer was caring for a sick parent and needed a four-day workweek, does that mean they cannot be promoted? Or be given important assignments? I would argue that under most circumstances they could, although many leaders in the workplace would pass them over.

The ebb and flow of these needs does not mean a lack of commitment. Nor do they reflect "mere" social issues. The realities of reproduction underpin our society and our economy. They are treated, to a degree, like they are "personal problems," rather than how we carry on the human race.

Does it make sense that the standard workday is 9:00 a.m. (or sometimes 8:00 a.m.) to 5:00 p.m. while the school day generally from 7:00 a.m. to 3:00 p.m.?

Women generally bear the brunt of this disconnect, even as they represent our greatest talent pool of leaders. Women are statistically more ambitious for leadership roles than men, being twice as likely to want to be promoted and earn senior-level leadership roles as their male colleagues. Our younger female workers are ambitious and hungry for leadership: two-thirds of women under thirty want to be senior leaders. These same younger women are more likely than the current slate of women leaders to prioritize flexibility. Few are willing to work mostly on-site. Thinking bigger and thus leading bigger with flexibility will unlock and empower both traditional and new sources of talent.

Yet we treat ambition and a desire for flexibility as mutually exclusive, stacking the deck against legions of women who want to lead. Who decided a senior leader has to be a workaholic, anyway? Why is that a good example, or healthy?

And work isn't just limited to that which is happening as an employee in your professional role. A 2023 Pew Research Center report points out that even as women's contribution to family income has grown over the past several years, those in opposite-sex marriages are *still* doing more housework and caregiving than men. In addition to this, there's "office housework" to contend with. Studies also show that women are more prone to take on these tasks and are more likely to be asked or tasked with doing them, such as arranging gatherings, note-taking, and various administrative, project management tasks.

There's also "office caregiving," which is work required to cultivate connection and culture, including mentoring, DEI initiatives such as employee groups, employee engagement activities, philanthropic work on behalf of the company, party planning, and more. In my experience and what research backs up is that women and multicultural people take on a disproportionate amount of office caregiving. While much of it may be passion and interest driven, this work doesn't usually garner reward or recognition, nor does it contribute to the advancement of those who do it. Professor Sanyin Siang of Duke University refers to them as invisible roles: "Often, they are not rewarded, incentivized, or even noticed—yet we keenly feel their absence." These roles do not come to life on a person's résumé or in their job description per se, but bigger leaders know that these roles are essential for both teams and cultures to thrive. Bigger leaders consciously consider, support, and recognize these contributors.

To have the most competitive and desirable advantage, you should be tapping into all the communities of talent, whether they be women, neurologically diverse people, multiple generations of workers, people with different educational backgrounds, or otherwise. You can't afford to leave big swaths of potential talent out of your search or to appear unwelcoming to both current and future employees. And so developing and sustaining a flexible workplace are key levers for attracting, retaining, and growing your people, now and increasingly in the future.

All this, including our declining TFR—which uniquely serves as both a lagging and a leading indicator—compels us to look very differently at our current workplace. In the words of Juliette Gordon Low, the founder of the Girl Scouts, "The work of today is the history of tomorrow, and we are its makers." Bigger leadership demands that we contemplate and own the consequences of our actions, not only for our generation, but for those to come.

CHAPTER TEN

FLEXIBILITY

FORTIFY YOUR CULTURE OF GROWTH

If you want to bend, not break, under pressure, you need flexibility in your people, practices, and policies. Bigger leaders champion flexible jobs, careers, and lives. They are rewarded with loyal, resilient employees who meaningfully contribute and larger talent pools to draw from.

E arly in my career, as I was looking to pivot from a technical role to one that was more business oriented, I interviewed with three different leaders who each had a product management job opening that interested me. I knew this move was going to be an important one, and I wanted to get a sense of the style of each of the leaders before making my final decision. I was leaning toward the most charismatic leader of the three, who also happened to be the youngest. From the outside, he seemed to be a magnet for other young, smart, dynamic people. But during my interview, I asked him about how he preferred to work with his direct reports, and he revealed that he would do one-on-one discussions only on Sundays. I tried to hide my shock and kept smiling as he went on to say that while he was available to his people, his regular workdays were packed to the brim with other urgencies, so Sunday was the perfect day to connect with his direct reports individually.

I left the meeting ruminating about what it would mean to work for him. No doubt I'd learn a lot. If I did well, I would likely garner his sponsorship for my career. His power and influence were growing across the company, and I could potentially become part of his inner circle. In the couple of days I had to decide, I scribbled countless lists of pros and cons for each of the roles. My head said to take the job with him, but I had a bad feeling in my gut. While I hadn't yet led people myself, it seemed bizarre to me that a leader would let their direct reports have meaningful one-to-one discussions with them only on Sundays. I'd risk unpredictable impacts to my Sundays for possibly years, being totally flexible for a boss who wouldn't adjust his calendar to meet the needs of his team.

Ultimately, I trusted my gut and declined the position with him, accepting a role working for a solid manager who respected the boundaries of weekends. This was absolutely the right choice for me at that time, as I was in such a formative part of my life as a young, single professional, wanting a successful launch into both a rewarding career and a rewarding life. Weekends belonged to me, not my employer.

My own interpersonal flexibility, a gift from my immigrant parents, who wanted nothing more than for me to fit in, was developed through every act of bullying, discrimination, microaggression, rejection, and alleged failure I encountered. These experiences built my grit and perseverance and literally helped me bounce back from setbacks, no matter how big. I trained myself to embody the common adage that "life is 10 percent what happens to you and 90 percent how you choose to react." Thus I focused more on what was possible, not on what had already happened, to show that I could do anything I set my mind to, albeit maybe not in the original way that I had thought.

And there's no doubt that this interpersonal flexibility underpinned my career advancement every step of the way. Early in my career, I determinedly pursued a sales role through six interviews over three years that yielded five rejections and one eventual yes. I learned a lot from those rejections. While my initial reaction was severe disappointment coupled with a big blow to my confidence, I later felt frustrated and even angry at times that I kept being turned down. After I worked through those emotions, I realized there were clearly reasons for why I was not the chosen candidate, and that I had an obligation to more fully understand the why. I had to widen my perspectives about what it took to secure one of these roles, such as direct leadership of a team and customer management experience. And I became a bigger leader through not only the career path that led me to sales, but from the experience itself, which largely shaped my view that one should always include the external world—customers, investors, competitors, suppliers, partners, industry analysts, communities, and more. I learned to focus both outside in (customer/market driven) and inside out (customer-centric/inclusive culture).

What got us here will not get us there. Leadership models of the past—low trust, low inspiration, high intimidation—no longer work in the face of this heightened complex connection. Revert to these methods in fear or from a mindset of scarcity, and you are playing small ball. Bigger leaders harness greater energy and win.

In this book we've covered a lot, and yes, leading bigger is . . . well, big. It means engaging with a wider group of stakeholders, taking the perspective of an increasingly diverse workforce, ensuring a workplace buoyed by a culture of belonging, and managing across changing workspaces.

The first chapter in this part covered the topic of safety, a foundational human need. The next shared thoughts about boundaries, which now blur and change for each individual.

Many of these concepts will come together in this chapter because they require one critical leadership skill that can make them possible: flexibility. We'll discuss flexibility in the workplace and workspaces, but this is all in the service of having an engaged workforce that accomplishes purpose-driven work.

A Framework for Flexibility

The concept of work-life balance has never quite set right with me; it implies your work is separate from your life. Work is simply one facet of your life. Do we talk about exercise-life balance, shopping-life or sleep-life balance? Even if any of these aspects might be out of control? Work is an integral part of your life, and increasingly, it's not separated from the other elements. Today people expect their leaders to understand that work is simply one part of their life, not their entire life. For years we've been chasing work-life balance, when in reality what matters most is flexibility. Flexibility in this context means the ability to adjust to shifting priorities that span both the professional and the personal realms.

I'm known to tell my people, "Life is an optimization equation," a phrase intended to emphasize the power of choosing your priorities. To solve this equation for yourself, you need to do three things: establish your priorities, use those priorities to guide your choices, and accept the consequences of those choices. I believe that you can have it all, just not all at the same time. Remember in chapter 7, when I "fell off" the high-potential track after deciding not to be geographically mobile. I was consciously aiming to keep my children near my parents. I knew intellectually it would harm my upward career progression, and it did. Then my priorities shifted again as my kids grew older, and as a family, we regrouped for a Texas adventure filled with growth. You'll know some consequences ahead of time; others will be unforeseen and may cause you to revisit your priorities.

So what does having a flexible workplace entail? And how should you, as a bigger leader, structure your workplaces in a flexible way? First, leaders must always recognize that an employee has a *job*, which is in the context of their *career*, which is ongoing, growing, and vital. Their career exists as a subset of their *life*—a significant part, but still simply a part of the vast landscape of one's life.

Let's start with the *job* part of the framework, the narrowest scope. A flexible workplace as it relates to somebody's job has to do with:

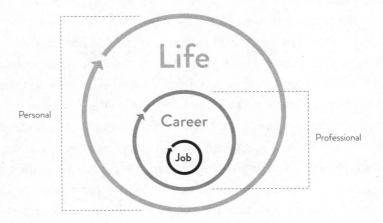

- Where do they work?

- How well do they work in terms of the different modalities and tools?

- When will they work? What is the workday?

- With whom do they work, and how will they do that?

- What resources do they need to get the job done?

We've seen a growing amount of experimentation across different companies about the where, the how, and even the when, including four-day workweeks and off-hours. With respect to the job, the bigger leader considers the different ways each individual can be most productive and engaged, as well as creative ways for the team to collaborate.

If you then expand to the context of their *career,* what does a flexible work environment mean? Employees are looking for growth, not only in their experiences or in the value they can add, but also in formal development such as education. In a flexible workplace, that could mean tuition-reimbursement programs or support for certifications that may help that individual beyond their current role and in their longer-term career. What career-development resources are available to your employees vis-à-vis their learning—book clubs, webinars, developmental programs? A flexible leader also considers sabbaticals and leaves if an individual desires to pursue other interests or take a break. A key aspect of supporting a person's career is the exposure you give them to a wide range of people, including those outside of your company, so they can cultivate relationships beyond their day-to-day colleagues.

Perhaps the most important context for a flexible workplace is the acknowledgment that someone's job and career exist in the context of their whole *life*. Embrace that people's lives always remain at the top of their mind. Perhaps they desire to have a partner, get married, or have children. Perhaps they are facing health problems or are caring for a loved one with major or chronic issues. Inclusive leaders acknowledge these life realities and milestones, taking on the responsibility to provide resources and benefits, ensuring that people can contribute to their jobs and have a thriving career even as their personal life evolves.

For all three elements, the key word related to flexibility is *choice*, as we established at the beginning of this section. I've said to many people, including my own kids, that your decisions and actions should focus on the creation of more choices, pathways, and options. The more we do this, the more in control we are and the more growth we can experience. Natural human behavior is such that when we lack choice, we tend to feel cornered, like a soon-to-be-defeated boxer in the ring. We feel less in control of our destiny. And no matter where you are in your job, career, or life, control matters for your overall well-being.

People like to speak of the workplace changes that occurred from 2020 to 2023 as "the new normal." I prefer to address "the *next* normal." We will continue to go through shifts that require our agility and flexibility. We are never done.

Technology is a main driver. Look at how whole business models have emerged from the widespread use of smartphones—everything from GPS mapping to ride-sharing, to the point where airports now have shuttles and designated areas to manage the traffic. As we move to 5G wireless, networks of cameras in cities, aided by AI, are already automating city services. For instance, city transportation systems can now harness tech created for first responders, and buses can be given green lights to speed transportation services in rush hour. This capability aids inclusion, as it can speed the path to work for those workers who rely on public transportation.

These tech-driven changes will only accelerate. For example, automation is removing the repetitive capture and analysis of financial data across large organizations. Generative AI is overtaking the entry-level writer and the first drafts of everything from website copy to social posts to legal briefs. Self-driving cars are shuttling passengers in San Francisco, and automated trucks are traversing Colorado every day.

What are the implications of those changes to your workplace? How will you help your workforce retrain? How can you be empathetic about the fear of technology taking livelihoods away?

Flexible Policies

Bigger leaders think differently about certain aspects of policy and practice. Sometimes human resources teams will mandate policies simply because that's how it's been done before, or it's the industry standard, or it's what is offered by the benefits platform used by the company. But companies can do better.

By this point in the book, it may come as no surprise that looking at the generational trends, we see that the younger generations don't just want flexible benefits, they expect them. Organizations simply must be intentional in how they develop and execute their benefits, like leaves, childcare and eldercare, vacation, health and well-being, or crisis care.

Health benefits. We've explored in Part 2 how bigger leaders focus on the entirety of somebody's well-being and their humanity. But in the past, healthcare benefits were generally limited to physical health.

The bigger leader looks at how policies support mental, emotional, and even financial well-being. This goes beyond what is included in the standard healthcare plan or employee assistance program. It can be sabbaticals, paternity leave, well-thought-out financial counseling with planning support, and creative incentives for going to the gym. Mercer's global survey of 14,000 employees found that "providing varied and valued benefits made those employees with access to the most varied well-being resources 35% less likely to move elsewhere, 27% more confident they can get the healthcare they need and 11% more energized."

Caregiving benefits. Having children, in my mind, is one of the greatest legacies people can leave. Of course that's not to say that everybody should have children or can have children or wants to have children. Bigger leaders will consciously support all their people, including support for life stages such as pregnancy and childbirth, considering new dynamics like surrogacy and fertility.

How are you defining a family? Two friends of mine, an LGBTQ+ couple, recently welcomed a child via surrogate. One spouse works for a company with generous parental leave. The other spouse was told that because she did not physically give birth, she's not entitled to any maternity leave. The traditional view of the two-gender nuclear family is both exclusionary and biased by nature. And companies should push to accommodate both parents, no matter their sexuality or gender. As the nature of families evolves, benefits and support should, too.

In that same vein, for those of us who may be pet lovers, our pets are members of our family. Some organizations provide support by subsidizing pet insurance for their people. Pets, like any loved one, affect our well-being, and their welfare affects ours. Growing up, I was one of those kids who never had a dog but always wanted one. So it seemed logical to me that when, as a newly married couple, we adopted our first dog, I would take an entire week off from work to ensure that he could acclimate. Looking back, I wish that I hadn't had to use my vacation to care for our furry new family member, and these days, more employers are offering benefits specifically related to pet care, to good effect: A third of pet owners are more likely to stay at their employer if offered pet insurance benefits, and the number climbs higher for Gen Z and millennial employees. The key, as it often is while leading bigger, is to remember that individual employees vary widely in how they value these benefits and that the future workforce is likely to shift the dynamics in a way that might surprise you. Whatever your personal beliefs and preferences, you'll need to flex accordingly.

Benefits specific to women's health. About fifteen years ago, I was having dinner with a dozen or so corporate executives from a variety of industries. I was engaged in a conversation with the lead executive at a large global manufacturing firm. We were discussing the talent and workforce pipeline, at which point he said, "Anne, I have encountered some amazing women in my career. The problem is that they get married and have babies." I was a bit taken aback, especially since his wife was present and he was the father of several daughters. I asked him to explain his point of view. He went on to say that when women get married, they're the ones who take time off to give birth and they're the ones who have to leave early to pick up the kid, and as such he found them to be less committed. I countered: "Don't you think the men would like to go see their child's soccer game as well? And maybe when the men leave, they're not actually telling you that they're going to go and see their kid's concert, but you have this perception that it's the women's role to do that." This reinforces the misconception that women should still take on a disproportionate amount of the caregiving for children and elders in their family. And this is despite the fact that women comprise upwards of 60 percent of college students, they're still taking on a disproportionate responsibility for the traditional family. That executive and I went on to have a lively, constructive conversation about this.

We must be extremely careful of our biases as well as those long embedded in processes, policies, and practices that are misogynistic and reflective of a patriarchy no longer relevant. We must be mindful of how we treat our people. No matter where you grew up or how you grew up, your job as the bigger leader is to eagerly expand your mind and understand the perspectives of the people you are supporting. Some people—often women and single parents—are the breadwinners *and* are also carrying the household. They are tired, pushed to the brink.

The inclusive, flexible workplace also acknowledges that childcare is a vital issue and a requirement for business and economic success—because its availability and accessibility enable the potential talent pool to expand, work, and thrive. Childcare support, whether in the form of on-premises facilities or stipends for emergency help, must be viewed as a must-have rather than a nice-to-have. Like the total fertility rate, childcare is not just a social or personal issue; it is one of critical economic importance.

This goes beyond pregnancy. Did you know that only a handful of countries in the world have formal laws for menstrual leave? Spain became the first European country to do so in early 2023, allowing workers who provide a doctor's note to take three to five days of leave a month if they suffer from cramps, nausea, dizziness, or vomiting. Similar laws exist in South Korea, Indonesia, Japan, Taiwan, and Zambia. Of note, Spain also passed several sexual and reproductive rights laws at the same time. Spain's total fertility rate has been below 2.1 since the 1980s.

I was talking to an executive about how her company proudly embraces inclusion as one of a growing number of companies in the United States who proactively addresses menopause. Did you know that more than a million Americans go through menopause each year, and many experience at least one severe symptom that affects their ability to do their job? These symptoms could include hot flashes, insomnia, mood swings, brain fog, and more. Her organization provides additional ergonomic support such as fans. They encourage working flex hours if the woman experiences symptoms during the day—and they understand that this is a natural stage of life as opposed to a taboo topic or one to be joked about and degraded.

In regard specifically to the workplace, having somewhere where new mothers can pump breast milk with some dignity is required by law. But too often it's still a closet or a bathroom stall. Please be careful if your family has made other choices, perhaps for the mother of children to stay home, when considering what to provide a new mother in the workplace. The period during the first year or so postpartum when new moms need to pump breast milk at work is difficult enough without enduring policies or practices arising from second-guessing women's decisions.

Our biases run deep. When I was on my second maternity leave, I vowed to take off a full six months versus the four I had taken after the birth of my first child. While I was away, there was a significant organizational restructuring. A new senior executive from outside the company was brought in with expectations that he would play a pivotal role. I got the call to come back early from leave to be his right-hand person. It was an exciting opportunity to learn from a dynamic power player, but I established some boundaries about my leave and agreed to help him from time to time, remotely until my return. While I was clear with HR and with the soon-to-be new boss, once I gave my conditional yes, the conditions were virtually forgotten. Because none of the leaders themselves had taken maternity leave, they had trouble understanding why I would rather give my baby a bath than be on a call with them! I remember having to gently educate them about the boundaries of my leave, as well as about the conditions of my remote role. Through this early tension, my candor, and my boss's willingness to listen, we built a strong relationship that got even stronger upon my in-person return. It was a good thing, because I lost count of the number of times my three-year-old got ahold of my BlackBerry and inadvertently sent him gibberish.

An inclusive organization must work diligently to provide flexibility to their employees across a myriad of life circumstances while not adversely affecting others. Transparently communicating the rationale and purpose of any given set of actions benefits the whole organization, and contributing to higher performance for all should be part of your playbook. Remember to ask yourself who *doesn't* benefit from this strategy, policy, or practice. How might you meet the needs of those who have other life situations?

Time away from work. Job security is always one of the biggest fears people have when they're away from work. Even when people are on official vacation, this fear exists in some fashion, such as the thought from the plane: *What if I fall behind? What if I'm not demonstrating my commitment and loyalty if I'm unreachable?* In my more than three decades of corporate work, I took my laptop with me on 99 percent of my vacations. I'm not proud of this fact. It wasn't good for my well-being or for my relationship with my family—and it was not appropriate behavior to model for my team.

A growing number of organizations have moved to a "take vacation whenever you need to" approach, also called unlimited paid time off (PTO), instead of allotting each employee a specified amount of vacation, whether based on tenure or otherwise. This approach signals that the organization prioritizes flexibility. But implementing this policy is a little more complicated. While I've never personally worked in an unlimited PTO environment, I have many friends who do, and they tell me that there are times when it's impractical because the needs of the business may trump vacations, and employees inconsistently use and sometimes abuse the policy.

Some companies put "unlimited time off" policies in place because it frees them from the administrative burden of managing vacation policies, and they find employees take much less vacation when given the ability to take it whenever they want. This is disingenuous and a recipe for burnout.

Perks. Your responsibility is to uncover what your people value, not necessarily what *you* value. Your employees might find it out of reach to get the latest gadget and would be delighted to be given it, or might want a ticket for the hot show in town and a nice hotel in your home city. Does that sound lavish? In the larger scheme of recruiting and retention costs, this is small potatoes. A smartwatch costs less than a LinkedIn ad to replace that worker.

As with many lead-bigger concepts, your policies and practices are there not just to support the people on your team *today,* but also to entice the people who will be on your team *tomorrow.* Policies that take into account that not everyone works the same way, that being tethered to a desk all day is not particularly healthy or productive, and that people want some control over how they work will make you much more attractive as an employer.

Not only will employees be proud to say they got their smartwatch as a professional recognition gift, but they will even more proudly cite the incredible support their company provides them to care for their well-being and performance in life. It might be that the bright team member who also happens to be on the autism spectrum finds tremendous relief doing great work remotely twice a week. Or the colleague that has anxiety performs best in the quiet early morning hours at the office, before others arrive, when they can get ahead. (But then their energy flags in the midafternoon, and they would be much more relaxed finishing the day's work at home). That entrepreneurial spirit who comes up with all of the great ideas? They might need to manage their own workload, and they will thrive if you remove bureaucratic obstacles to their success.

Whether it's financial wellness or professional growth, if an organization embraces every person and their goals authentically, not only will people feel that they belong, but they will also want to.

Elevated cultures always pay handsome dividends to those who know how to care for their people, helping them deliver to their fullest potential. In times of uncertainty, gritty, flexible organizations win.

Though I've suggested several tangible practices to consider in this chapter, what we are creating is agility. No one leadership tactic will solve for organizational and individual agility in an ever-changing business landscape. What people need to perform at their best today may not work tomorrow. As researchers at McKinsey write, "Think of flexibility not as an end point but as a set of evolving expectations." Bigger leaders, who take a wider perspective in service of having a greater impact, will thrive in these dynamic times.

Lead Bigger Embodying Flexibility

- How often are policies and practices around flexibility assessed and updated in your organization?

- Which flexible policies or practices do your employees value most? Which ones are they asking for? What is the rationale for not implementing those policies or practices?

- How do you personally view employees who take leave? Do you find some types of leave valid and others not? How might your employees be affected by your views?

- Look down the road at your future workforce. Can you anticipate any changing expectations or even demands around workplace flexibility? How will your team/organization adjust?

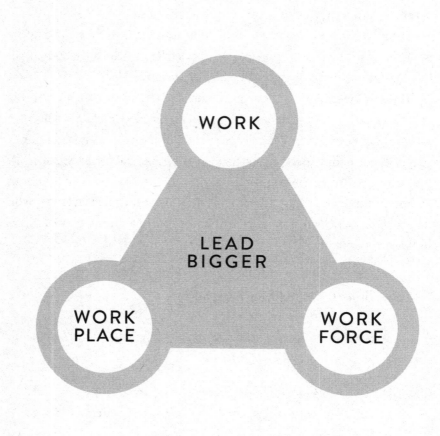

PART FOUR

BIGGER
CONVERSATIONS

This final section includes conversations that are about widening your perspective to have a greater impact: gaining additional perspectives to help us expand our understanding as we implement the mindsets and practices discussed throughout.

When I first set out to write this book, I knew it was important to get direct and diverse insights from experts who have both studied and practiced inclusive leadership. I wanted to feature voices of several people who are viewed as key thought leaders on leadership as a whole. I specifically chose three from very different backgrounds to get their views on the importance of inclusive leadership based on their own unique experiences, discoveries, and learnings. In each conversation, it's clear that the imperatives of leading bigger and inclusion transcends every role and can be applied quite universally in any context. For **GENERAL STANLEY MCCHRYSTAL,** inclusion means attracting the best people to build the best-performing organization, and **ARIANNA HUFFINGTON** emphasizes how leaders must embed moments of belonging in everyday culture. We don't know how the future will unfold, but as **ADAM GRANT** predicts, inclusion will be a requirement regardless of how the world changes.

I am grateful for their willingness to share their time, wisdom, and leadership. I hope you enjoy their insights as much as I enjoyed our discussions.

CHAPTER ELEVEN

"IF YOU WANT TO WIN"

A CONVERSATION WITH
GENERAL STANLEY MCCHRYSTAL

I had the privilege of speaking with General Stanley McChrystal about the challenges and opportunities of leading bigger in a traditional hierarchical environment. His perspective is that inclusive leadership is essential for dealing with the uncertainties leaders are facing in today's environment.

First, can you talk about a time that you felt a sense of belonging that had a profound effect in your work or personal life?

McChrystal: I had an experience where I did three years in a job and had three different bosses. I was a major at the time, so I wasn't new to the Army, but those three different bosses had very different styles. It was a very elite counterterrorist organization. But it was fascinating, almost like a study. The first year I was there, the leader of the section I was in was very inclusive. He wasn't considered as highly as some other leaders, but he was incredibly inclusive. I felt like I was a valued member of the team, and I worked my rear end off. The second year, they brought in a guy to replace him in a one-year tour in a key job. This guy was more of an elitist, not only by view of the military, but by view of the people he hung around. So inside the section we operated, there were people in the in-crowd and people in the out-crowd. Suddenly for the second year, I felt as though I was not a member of the team. I had the same job, I was doing the same hard work, but when the cool guys got in a room to talk about cool guy stuff, I wasn't invited in.

The third year we got a guy who was not as good as either of the first two in terms of technical competence or connection to the senior people. But he was incredibly inclusive. And so it was back to that first-year experience, where suddenly I felt more valued. I worked harder, my morale was higher. It was a whipsaw effect, but it was a great way to remind me how someone in my role feels when it's good and when it's not good. That variable changed my outlook on the job completely.

What happens if leaders don't evolve to an inclusive style of leadership?

McChrystal: In the civilian world, if you make a lot of money or get political power, or in the military, if you're senior in rank, you start to surround yourself at the closest level with people who make you comfortable. They may be people like you with a certain personality trait. They may be the good old boy network or people who belong to the same club. But that leader becomes more and more insulated by the people they include because those people have access.

At Yale, I teach C. S. Lewis's essay "The Inner Ring," and the whole argument is that we have a natural hunger to be included in the in-crowd, to get in that inner ring. But the inner ring isn't special unless someone is excluded. There's no point in being in an elite club if everybody can be in it. That brings out the worst in us. We're happy to be in the inner ring because it's special. Leaders get fewer perspectives. They get an echo chamber and huge resentment from parts of the organization whose talents aren't leveraged and whose loyalty isn't engendered.

Let's pivot to some of the ways that you personally practice inclusion.

McChrystal: I learned these ideas from great people, I didn't invent any of them. The first was basic communication, when I commanded a large counterterrorist task force during the war in Iraq particularly, but also in Afghanistan. With the nature of a chain of command and information passage, typically at the top level, you have a small meeting, then information cascades down the various levels through the force. We found out that wasn't fast enough. So we put everybody on the same video teleconference every day, and it ended up being 7,500 people. And you say, that's madness. Obviously 7,500 people aren't talking, but now you've opened up what used to be the inner sanctum conversation. So not only do they hear directly what senior people are saying, they can ask questions and start to interact.

The first thing you do is democratize information, because in hierarchical systems, the cascading of information means filtering. It's not always intentional, but it has that effect and it gets corrupted. We created what we called *shared consciousness* to get information to everybody. If everybody has a common ability to hear the same thing at the same time, you level the playing field to a degree.

The second thing was just the physical layout of how we operated our command centers. When we started, there were little rabbit warrens. There would be a part of the command center where certain things got done, but then adjacent offices were locked off to people, partly for security reasons, but partly culture. Our force would get a little set of offices and block everybody else out because they could. We opened all that up. We brought everybody on the main floor. And it created interactions between people through constant contact. In the military, they always talk about "behind the green door" where the secret stuff occurs. The reality is, there are a couple places where you have to do that for certain classified stuff, but the rest, you can bring it out, air it out, and share it.

That starts to tell people we're all at a common level. We had a task force that included civilians from different agencies—Department of State, National Security Agency, CIA—and was part military, part civilian agencies. We ran a two-week course to teach them how to operate so that they didn't feel like a lesser person, like a freshman in college who didn't know where to get food. We brought them into alignment as much as possible.

Now it's still hard work because in the counterterrorist forces, the commandos are at the top of the structure, and they've got a hulking physical presence and relationships that go back decades. They have inside jokes and trust. You have to get people shoulder to shoulder and as much as possible, open that up. That isn't simple—you don't do it with just a directive, but by a number of steps. Making cross-functional teams where you put people from different entities together, familiarity did not bring contempt. It bred respect for the fact that people of different backgrounds had a contribution. It took time for that meritocracy to come through.

At face value, inclusive leadership and traditional hierarchical leadership seem to be at odds. How does hierarchy live with inclusion, and how can that be done constructively and fruitfully?

McChrystal: It's a learned skill because they may not be in opposition, but they're at least in tension. For example, we had six levels of the chain of command in that particular organization. Part of each leader's power derived from the fact that they controlled the flow of information down and up, and they decided what the people below them get and the quality control of the information going up. The problem is in a complex, fast-moving environment, that's too slow and there's too much filtering. So we opened up the information.

The question for the leaders in the middle was "If I don't control that information, am I responsible if junior people pass bad information because we're in such a hurry or if they don't understand?" And my response was "Yes, you are." We pushed decision-making authority lower as well, not for everything, but we pushed as low as we could. And then that middle part says, "Wait a minute, if I'm not making the decision, am I still responsible for the outcome? That's not fair." And we said, "We're not deciding whether it's fair or not—this is the way it's going to be. What you can do is develop your people. You make them more prepared to make the decision that they have to make to be fast enough. You work on their understanding of information. You are a shaper now, when you used to be a gatekeeper."

It took a lot of time and interaction for those middle-level leaders to understand where their value-add was and how to live with what they felt was the risk of being held responsible for things they didn't completely control. That's something I think businesses just have to come to grips with.

You're a self-described old white guy. What would you say to other old white guys about why inclusion is an essential leadership competency and not a political trend? What do they stand to gain from the risk and change of this approach?

McChrystal: So the first thing I'd say is, if you were leading an army that was fighting against an army of similar demographics—let's say the Civil War, where your army is American white guys and you're fighting against an army of American white guys—there's not a big requirement to change. Inclusion is not the variable in that particular case that was likely to be dominant and make a difference.

But several things have happened, and we've had to learn first. Our competition is leveraging more and more talent and meaning. They're leveraging diversity. Terrorist groups use women, kids, old people, and it gives them effectiveness. Also, my peers, the old white guys, are leading forces that are more diverse. And you have to get as much performance out of that group as you possibly can. You can't fence off and protect the demographics so you just have the people that you want. The reality is, if you want to get as much talent as possible, you're going to have to go diverse, which means you have to lead a diverse group, which means you probably have to change the way you communicate. You certainly have to change the way that you think.

When we formed the McChrystal Group twelve and a half years ago, I had several other guys with experience with me. We brought in young people and different backgrounds. In some ways, it was funny because we overcompensated. We said, "Well, we're in the civilian world now, where everybody sits on beanbag chairs and calls each other by their first names." We walked on eggshells around everybody, and it was well intentioned. We were trying to be the leaders we thought we needed to be. What we forgot is that leaders still must have high expectations, clear standards. You could push anybody hard to get the mission done. You just have to be fair.

So we've had this journey where it took us quite a while to figure out there's a core of basic leadership, getting the job done. Values that have nothing to do with gender or age or race or any of that. Everybody wants to be on a team that gets it done.

How do you deal with the resisters to inclusivity, who are perhaps having a toxic effect on the team?

McChrystal: The problem is those resisters might be really, really good at what they do—your best salesperson or your best operator. The first thing is you have to demand high standards. If you start lowering the standards for the outcome just to push inclusion, you're going to have a lot of resentment.

Forcing them to do some things together is pretty powerful. We created cross-functional teams where we put together different entities. They didn't get a choice: This is who you get, make it work. I think that familiarity is probably the most important part of that. Units, particularly elite organizations, will almost demand the ability to select the talent they want. If they select in a nondiverse way, this is a hard one, because you have to convince them. If you mandate it, then you've given them an excuse not to get the outcome you are demanding, and they can hide behind that. I don't have a clever way except we created cross-functional teams, we put liaisons, we did as much as we could, but it was always hard.

Your biggest piece of advice is to force exposure and familiarity in hopes of learning and growth, because the resister's natural inclination will be to avoid it at all costs.

McChrystal: And you have to demonstrate that behavior. Because if you don't do it, then you're saying one thing and doing another, and they'll pick that up in a heartbeat.

Trust is usually easier and more comfortable to build in homogeneous environments. How do you build trust in teams that prioritize differences? Because it's harder to relate to somebody who is different from you, but trust is foundational to the performance of the team, to the realization of the mission.

McChrystal: I think that the only way to get trust is to get experience with something. If you went to the same school as someone, even if you weren't there at the same time, you say, "That person went to my school, so there is lower risk of extending my trust to them." We have to create interactions for that, but you also have to give people common experiences. A male colonel is likely to trust a female colonel because they've been through a certain amount of stuff. It's creating shared or common credentials. The real gold standard is of course interaction with individuals themselves, to get to know them, but scaling that is hard. You can create relationships between certain people in organizations, and that to a degree can extrapolate. Because if I know one person from that organization, I'm likely to say, "I trust them. Therefore I can give a certain level of trust to anybody from that organization."

What's the risk if we don't move to inclusive leadership in more facets of society: economy, technology, politics?

McChrystal: We're in an extraordinarily competitive world. I'll take the warfare part. If you went back to ancient times, the strength of an army was about how strong your arms and shoulders were. Nowadays, war is very different. It's fought with technology. So that's not the metric of power of an individual soldier or cumulatively of an army. Let's say you are using white males only. Well, in the United States, when you're cutting out 17 percent African American and other minorities, you're taking your pool down. Then you cut all females out. You're trying to field the most capable organization from 27 or 28 percent of the population. That's really high risk. If we expand that to a nation and we say we're in a very competitive environment, economically, politically, diplomatically, militarily, we can't afford to leave any talent unleveraged.

This is an emotional issue for some people, and I get that. But I come at it in a very practical sense. If you want to win, this is what you have to do.

Stanley McChrystal, a retired four-star general, is the former commander of U.S. and International Security Assistance Forces Afghanistan and the former commander of the nation's premier military counterterrorism force, Joint Special Operations Command. Throughout his military career, his command included more than 150,000 troops from forty-five allied countries. Stanley is a senior fellow at Yale University's

Jackson Institute of Global Affairs, serves on numerous boards, including FiscalNote and JetBlue Airways. He is also the New York Times *bestselling author of* My Share of the Task *and* Team of Teams: New Rules of Engagement for a Complex World. *He is also founder, partner, CEO, and chairman of McChrystal Group, a global consultancy focused on delivering innovative leadership solutions around the world.*

CHAPTER TWELVE

"TAKING A WHOLE-HUMAN APPROACH TO WELL-BEING"

A CONVERSATION WITH ARIANNA HUFFINGTON

Leaders are facing a daunting expectation to consider their workforce more broadly than ever before: zooming out from the day-to-day job to see them in the context of their careers and lives. In my conversation with wellness expert Arianna Huffington, she argues that this bigger approach to leading your workforce will reward you many times over, from better shareholder value and higher performance to the meaning that comes from acting out of our highest values.

Tell us about a time you felt included or a sense of belonging that had a profound effect on your work or life.

Huffington: When I was at Cambridge University, I was fascinated by the Cambridge Union, the university's debating society. I was thrilled by how the power of words and rhetoric could be marshaled to persuade and change people's minds and hearts. So I joined. The only problem was that I had a thick Greek accent, which I was deeply insecure about and for which

I was constantly teased. At the end of my first year, while I was away in London for a weekend, a friend nominated me to be on the Union standing committee—the first step on the Union career ladder. When I returned to Cambridge and found out, I was aghast, convinced I wouldn't get a single vote. But the ballots had been printed and I couldn't get my name removed. To my complete surprise, I got the most votes for the post. That was the beginning that led in my third year to my being elected the third female—and first foreign—president of the Union. It was an important lesson for me about the power of belonging. Until then, I had believed I didn't belong, and that belief was constantly reinforced by my own self-talk—what I call the obnoxious roommate living in my head. I had to shift that belief and silence that voice to see that in fact I did belong as much as anybody else. As a result, I lost much of my insecurity—though none of my accent!

Who has been an inclusive leader in your life?

Huffington: Thrive Global's chief training officer Joey Hubbard has been a role model to me on what inclusive leadership means. That's also why he's the host of our course on inclusion called "Thriving Belonging." In one section, he tells his own story, which is a powerful lesson on inclusion and why it also has to include an inner journey. He talks about growing up in South Central Los Angeles and the mindset shift he had to make, reframing limiting beliefs within himself to finally feel like he belonged. As he says, "All the external changes in the world won't make a difference if we as individuals feel that we are impostors, unworthy, or don't belong."

What will happen if leaders don't evolve to an inclusive style of leadership?

Huffington: Diversity, equity, inclusion, and belonging have to be top priorities for leaders who want their organization to be competitive. A recent study showed that the top three reasons employees gave for leaving their jobs are not feeling valued by the company, not feeling valued by their leaders, and not feeling a sense of belonging. In today's marketplace, leaders can't afford not to tap into the largest possible talent pool. Inclusion brings more voices to the table and drives creativity and innovation. And inclusion isn't just about driving shareholder value—though countless studies show it certainly does that—it's also about acting on our highest values.

What are some of the most important ways you practice inclusion?

Huffington: One of our core values at Thrive is what we call compassionate directness. It means empowering employees to speak up, disagree, and surface problems and pain points in real time and in an open way. And then encouraging others to do the same. It's how we create a thriving culture instead of letting resentments fester.

In our hiring process at Thrive, we dedicate a specific interview round to a conversation about our cultural values. But the key is to shift our mindset from hiring based on culture fit to culture *add*. Hiring solely based on cultural fit can lead to groupthink and hamper innovation as a company grows. Instead, we try to look for new perspectives that a candidate can add to our culture. This can also mean looking beyond career history and work experience, which can work against candidates from underrepresented communities, and focusing also on curiosity and willingness to learn and grow.

How are inclusion and employee well-being related?

Huffington: Empathy is at the core of inclusion. And when we're stressed and burned out, our capacity for empathy is also depleted. That's why it's so important to embed moments of belonging into everyday culture.

At Thrive, we're actively developing ways to do this using our behavior change platform, and one of my favorites is Thrive Reset. In the Thrive platform, users can create and share their own personalized Reset. You can select photos of your loved ones, pets, holidays and celebrations, along with music you love and quotes that are meaningful to you.

It's like a sixty-second window into what's important in your life and what gives you joy— and it's a powerful engine for connection and empathy.

At Thrive, we start every team meeting with a different person sharing their Reset. It's a great way to foster connections and make sure everyone feels seen and heard.

You've been working on the intersection between well-being and leadership for quite some time. What are the most profound changes that have emerged in your advice over the past five years? What are the most important trends that you anticipate will surface in the next five years?

Huffington: How we think about both burnout and well-being have undergone a profound change in recent years. Bragging about burnout is no longer seen as the badge of honor it was only a few years ago. And much of that is due to the increasing acceptance of the science of how humans recharge and achieve peak performance. I think of it as a human energy revolution. It's about acknowledging the truth that life should not revolve around work but around our full humanity, which includes work but also includes nurturing our health and well-being, our relationships, our capacity for wonder and joy and for giving back.

At the same time, well-being has gone from being thought of as a perk to an essential strategy for success. One of the biggest tasks ahead of us is to continue to solidify this trend and lock in these gains, even in the midst of uncertainty—because it's in challenging times when we most need to double down on well-being and resilience.

How are inclusive leaders better equipped to anticipate, address, and embrace those trends?

Huffington: Being a good leader means being able to see the icebergs—before they sink your ship. That means being open to all voices and all perspectives. Leading an organization with inclusion as a core value means that the organization is going to be better able to anticipate challenges and more resilient to meet them.

As the workforce becomes increasingly diverse, how do inclusive leaders effectively address well-being when it's so individualized and personal? How do they prioritize their focus?

Huffington: Creating a culture of well-being starts at the top. It's like what they say on airplanes: put your own oxygen mask on first before helping others. When leaders are seen to prioritize their own well-being, not only does it make them more effective at everything they do, it also gives others permission to do the same.

Too many leaders still buy into the misguided notion that urgent or chaotic times require them to be in constant motion and always on, or that they somehow have to match the frenetic pace of the moment. In fact, the opposite is true. It is judgment that we need from leaders in times of uncertainty, not just stamina.

As younger generations enter the workforce, inclusive leaders must become more attuned to the growing mental health crisis. What should these leaders be aware of and how should they evolve their leadership practice to most effectively support this workforce?

Huffington: It's clear that the younger generations now entering the workforce are profoundly shifting the conversation on mental health in the workplace. They talk about mental health more openly, and they're much more likely to reject the myth that burnout and poor mental health are simply the price we have to pay for success. This is being driven by young people, but it's a shift everybody is going to benefit from. Forward-thinking leaders who value inclusivity will act on this by taking a whole-human approach to well-being.

Part of bringing our whole selves to work means that we no longer feel like we're supposed to check our emotions or experiences or mental health challenges at the door.

And leaders need to be aware of how events outside the workplace might affect people differently. For instance, for Black Americans, police killings result in 1.7 more poor mental health days. This doesn't mean leaders should pry or make broad assumptions. But you can be alert. And that will help you spot the warning signs if someone on your team is struggling. It's an opportunity to provide real-time and ongoing support that will benefit both employees and the organization as a whole.

How do you see this epidemic of burnout playing out globally? How can inclusive leaders who support global teams incorporate well-being practices across their multicultural workforce?

Huffington: The burnout epidemic is indeed global, which is why the World Health Organization added burnout to its *International Classification of Diseases and Related Health Problems* in 2019. And the move to globally distributed hybrid workforces, which was greatly accelerated by the pandemic, has shown that well-being has to be a core part of company culture, not something that's tied to physical offices. That means meeting employees where they are.

A tool Thrive has created for our partners is the Daily Check-In, which is the entry point to Thrive's platform. It's a daily question for employees that prompts a moment of reflection delivered via the platforms they're already using, like Microsoft Teams or Slack. There are dozens of different questions, some about personal well-being, some about work—including their feelings of belonging at work. Depending on the employee's response, Thrive offers personalized Microsteps and content recommendations.

Based on hundreds of thousands of daily conversations with employees around the world, here are some of the key insights Thrive has gathered on inclusion:

- 92 percent say that they "welcome feedback about how I treat others."

- 87 percent say that "it is my responsibility to make my workplace welcoming to everyone."

- 74 percent can "think of concrete examples of when I have taken action to support a colleague, friend, or family member of a different culture."

- 68 percent can "think of times I've spoken up for other people."

- 57 percent feel "comfortable asking my coworkers about their unique personal cultures and customs."

You have been known to say that in the human operating system, downtime is a feature and not a bug. What paradigm shifts, policy changes, and workforce practices would you alter to drive breakthroughs in support of this belief (workweek, vacation, etc.)?

Huffington: As we've seen throughout history, the culture doesn't always shift when the science does. We've had the science on human energy, burnout, and our need for downtime for decades. The pioneering work of researchers like Christina Maslach and Herbert Freudenberger dates back to the mid-1970s.

But societies don't roll out the welcome mat for theories that challenge the status quo. We still have a lot of work to do for our culture to fully catch up to the science of how we perform at our best and thrive in all aspects of our lives. Yes, well-being benefits like vacation policy will be a part of that, but what's really required is rethinking how we work and live.

What are the two or three things every inclusive leader should do to support their people's well-being?

Huffington: One thing an inclusive leader can do is to acknowledge that both inclusion and well-being must include an inner journey. It's up to all of us to create workplaces that value well-being and inclusion. At the same time, we have to accept that we're all going to make mistakes. So making space for grace, growth, and learning is essential. I love the concept of *wince moments,* a term coined by psychologist John Amaechi. It's when you catch yourself saying something embarrassing or even potentially offensive. These moments happen to all of us. But how we respond matters. We need to own up to our mistakes. But we also need to strip away the guilt and shame so that wince moments can become teachable moments. As leaders, we can create cultures that encourage these teachable moments.

Adopting compassionate directness as a core value helps embed well-being into the fabric of company culture. Another valuable well-being tool we use at Thrive is the entry interview. It's a conversation between the new hire and their manager. The first question is: "What's important to you in your life *outside* of work and how can we support you?" And to keep their connection strong, managers and employees revisit this initial entry interview conversation during their regular one-on-ones.

Arianna Huffington is the founder and CEO of Thrive Global, the founder of The Huffington Post, *and the author of fifteen books. In 2016, she launched Thrive Global, a behavior change technology company with the mission of improving productivity and health outcomes.*

She has been named to Time *magazine's list of the world's 100 most influential people and the Forbes Most Powerful Women list. Originally from Greece, she moved to England when she was sixteen and graduated from Cambridge University with an MA in economics. Her last two books,* Thrive: The Third Metric to Redefining Success and Creating a Life of Well-Being, Wisdom, and Wonder *and* The Sleep Revolution: Transforming Your Life, One Night at a Time, *both became instant international bestsellers. Most recently, she wrote the foreword to Thrive Global's first book,* Your Time to Thrive: End Burnout, Increase Well-Being, and Unlock Your Full Potential with the New Science of Microsteps.

CHAPTER THIRTEEN

"IF YOU'RE NOT INCLUSIVE, YOU'RE NOT A LEADER"

A CONVERSATION WITH ADAM GRANT

As the workplace continues to change around us, the winning leader of the future is the flexible thinker, someone willing to listen, empathize, take in new and challenging information, and respond. Adam Grant, an organizational psychologist at Wharton, not only studies the profound benefits of flexible thinking but strives to model it himself.

Could you share a time when you felt included and a deep sense of belonging that had a profound effect on your work or your life?

Grant: The first defining moment was when I was a freshman in high school. I showed up at tryouts for diving, and I was terrible. At the end of the tryout, the coach, Eric Best, said, "I will never cut a diver who wants to be here." He welcomed me onto the team and proceeded to tell me that he would put in as much time to help me grow as I put in. In the off-season, Eric volunteered his own personal time to coach me after school and never charged me a dime, and I felt extremely valued. I felt like I belonged to a team even though I wasn't any good. That was a huge part of motivating me to want to become good, so Eric wasn't wasting the investment he made in me—I wanted him to be successful.

It is such a great example of something you have always reinforced, which is the importance of hiring and focusing on people based on their will and attitude as opposed to purely their skill and experience. There's definitely something there that modern leadership can embrace more amply. So beyond Eric, who clearly was a formative inclusive leader in your life, is there someone else who has also been a formative or a pivotal inclusive leader?

Grant: One I had the privilege of working with for a long time was my colleague Sigal Barsade. When I first came to Wharton, Sigal was our area coordinator. She decided who taught what and led our hiring. I was new and inexperienced, and she was a star teacher, but when I came in to teach a class that she and our colleague Nancy Rothbard had developed, they invited me to design part of the class. They asked, "What do you love to teach? What ideas and approaches do you want to incorporate?" They not only included me from day one, they actually empowered me to shape the design of the class. I was stunned that I was being given that much responsibility and trust, and I really felt valued from the day I arrived here.

What happens if leaders don't evolve to an inclusive style of leadership? What is the counter to that in terms of what you've seen or what you've experienced?

Grant: The evidence is strong that leaders lose when they fail to be inclusive. It's not just something that's beneficial to the people that you manage. It's actually vital to the success and survival of organizations. We know that when leaders aren't inclusive, they don't hear problems and therefore can't solve them. They leave people biting their tongues instead of sharing their ideas. They leave people feeling less motivated. And at the end of the day, your best talent has the most options and is the most likely to leave. So you're basically failing in leadership if you fail to include people.

Those are powerful examples, and in my view, inclusion has to become a core competency going forward. For most people, inclusion is table stakes now; it's not even optional. Whereas before when we were perhaps more siloed or walled off or there were lots of people who were like us, we could be successful that way. It's not that way anymore. The diversification and complexity are growing in terms of the market and the world.

Grant: I think you're spot-on. For a podcast *Is It Safe to Speak Up?* I talked with Admiral William McRaven about encouraging people to raise problems and propose solutions, and including them in decisions. And he said, "You got all these names for it, but in the military, we just called it leadership." What a clear statement that inclusion is table stakes. If you're not inclusive, you're not a leader.

What are some of the most important ways that you practice inclusion, either professionally or personally? How do you live the practice of being an inclusive leader?

Grant: I don't want to assume that I live it, because that's in the eye of the beholder. You'd have to ask people who work with me whether I succeed or not. I can tell you how I strive for it. Whenever somebody works with me, I let them know that one of my core principles is I don't want there to be any gap between what you would say behind my back and what you feel comfortable saying to my face. If you have feedback or constructive criticism to help me improve, if you have a concern or a question that would help you, I expect you to voice it.

I try to open that door by following some of the research I did with Constantinos Coutifaris, by actually criticizing myself out loud and saying, "Here are some of the things that I'm bad at, that I'm working to improve. What do you think of these areas? Tell me if you've noticed other ways I can get better at that I'm not seeing yet, which might be blind spots for me."

I sometimes have to do it repeatedly. I actually had a call earlier today with a collaborator whose constructive criticism made it to me via a colleague. It was really valuable to me, so I reached out and said, "This is something I need to work on. Here's how I'm trying to work on it. And I would love to know what I can do to make sure I hear it directly from you next time." Their response was: "I just thought you would be too busy. And I didn't think I had anything important to say." I clarified that "I'm never too busy to hear something that might help me improve or help me help someone else. If you see something that you think might be relevant, let me judge whether it's important. Don't make that judgment for me." So that's an effort on my part to be inclusive, and whether it's effective is not for me to judge.

In the example you gave, the words that struck me were the requirement and the desire for total transparency, to build trust in that environment or in that relationship, your desire to be proactively vulnerable. In my opinion, that's absolutely something that inclusive leaders do, and it's something that many leaders don't do well, because it's super uncomfortable. It's super uncomfortable to say, "I don't even know what that thing means" or "I don't know what that acronym stands for. I actually don't even know how to get started." The vulnerability of this, of admitting our blind spots and our weaknesses, is something that pulls people in, but it has to be done repeatedly. I found people don't even believe that you're saying it sometimes. They think it's a trick.

Grant: You're so right. Over the years I've gotten a fair number of comments along the lines of "You're vulnerable in admitting your failures. You opened your first TED talk with your failure to invest in Warby Parker." I didn't start doing that in front of big public audiences. I started sharing those failures in the classroom because I was trying to relate to students on a human level and show them that I had lots of flaws and I wasn't going to judge them for being imperfect because I'm imperfect. I felt like the best way to establish vulnerability in the classroom was to model it. Teaching and leadership are very similar that way. You have to set the tone. If you're not vulnerable, the people around you won't be, either.

One of the challenges of being human is that we get set in our ways, our perspectives, and our biases, based on our own experiences and what we've absorbed. Your research and your point of view around rethinking are so powerful. One of the opening assertions in this book is there is a real-life challenge about this word inclusion: It's been bounded by DEI, but it's so much more. It is actually what modern leadership requires. What do you feel leaders need to do in terms of rethinking inclusion?

Grant: Fundamentally, inclusion is about enabling every person to feel valued, not just for their contributions to the organization, but as a human being. And that involves giving them a sense of belonging, saying, "You matter here, and you matter to me." There's some research on this by So-Hyeon Shim, Robert Livingston, Kathy Phillips, and Simon Lam: One of the most basic drivers of people feeling valued and included is just how often the leader looks at them. Literally just being looked at makes you feel seen. It's more than a metaphor.

That's been one of the challenges of virtual and hybrid work for a lot of people: You don't really know if anybody's looking at you. One of the fun ways I've tried to navigate that in Zoom meetings is sending individual messages in the chat: "Hey, I would love to hear your thoughts on this." I want to make it clear that I care about what they have to say, and I see them as individuals, even though I have to look at my camera instead of their face.

The opposite of inclusion is exclusion. And that means you are left out of important conversations. It means you can't voice your ideas. It means you are going to be pushed to the margin, i.e., marginalized. And that's a really poor way to lead people. So I think we need to think about how to help everyone feel included—not just as part of our DEI initiatives, but as a core leadership skill.

The whole reality of caring for the whole human, leading the whole human, supporting the whole human beings brings today's managers and tomorrow's leaders into some uncomfortable space, really up front and close with personal and professional boundaries. How would you guide or advise the inclusive leader to manage those boundaries, as it relates to supporting the whole person?

Grant: There's not a one-size-fits-all solution. One of the most critical steps a leader can take is to recognize that people vary in what Nancy Rothbard calls preferences for integration versus segmentation. Integrators are very happy to blur the line between work and the rest of life. They're excited to bring their kids to work. They have pictures of their family at the office. They invite their colleagues over for dinner, maybe even on vacation. And they don't want a personal-professional divide.

The group we have to be much more thoughtful with is segmenters, who Nancy shows are less satisfied and less committed in organizations with integrating policies. For example, it really bothers segmenters if there's on-site childcare in an organization. Even if their kids aren't there, they don't think children belong in the workplace. And they want to disconnect after work—they don't necessarily want to go to company parties. As a leader, it's important to understand the integrating versus segmenting preferences of the people you work with. And if you're going to do bonding or team-building or community-building, try to come up with events that are not just catered to the integrators. As you set your policies, make sure you're supporting the preferences of segmenters—who actually have higher well-being on average. Even integrators need to learn to set boundaries and segment.

In my early days in the corporate world, I used to say that the most important characteristic as a leader was interpersonal flexibility, for the reasons you're saying. Because the leader has to be the one who flexes all the time to their people. On a final note, what do you think the workplace is going to look like ten years from now?

Grant: It's always a risky proposition to try to predict the future. I love the old joke that historians aren't even that good at predicting the past. But one thing I'm excited about for the future is that there's going to be an increasing premium on inclusive leadership. Rightfully, talent has gained more power. Employees have more say, in part because it's easier for them to get a job anywhere than it was in the past. And I think that's only going to continue as a trend. It's likely then that leaders who fail at inclusion will struggle even more than they currently do at attracting, motivating, innovating, and retaining people. That will make inclusive leadership a must-have, not just a nice-to-have. That would be one prediction about the future of work that I feel comfortable making, with the recognition that I might be wrong. And if I am, I will be ready to think again.

Adam Grant is an organizational psychologist at Wharton and a bestselling author who explores the science of motivation, generosity, original thinking, and rethinking. He has been recognized as one of the world's ten most influential management thinkers and one of Fortune's *40 under 40. He is the number one* New York Times *bestselling author of six books that have sold millions of copies and been translated into forty-five languages:* Hidden Potential, Think Again, Give and Take, Origi-nals, Option B, *and* Power Moves. *Adam hosts the TED podcasts* Re:Thinking *and* WorkLife. *Adam earned his PhD in organizational psychology from the University of Michigan and his BA from Harvard University.*

CONCLUSION
ADVANCING THE
LEAD BIGGER MOVEMENT

B igger leaders are needed now more than ever to provide a wider view of the use and implications of technology for our work, workforce, and workplace. This is a critical time for leaders to lean into their humanity, inspiring their teams while helping the individuals around them safely steer their careers in meaningful and fulfilling ways.

Leading small is a style from the past that no longer works. The interdependent world, coupled with emerging technologies, simply does not permit small, selfish behavior. At the very least, leading small means you can't compete with leaders who can bring along an entire army of inspired stakeholders. At the worst, it leads to scandal and catastrophe.

If you've come this far, then you know: In a complex and interconnected world, leading bigger creates sizable competitive advantages, activating greater performance around a singular impactful purpose. You will be better able to rally the people who matter and win trust in an environment that provides high psychological safety and a culture of belonging.

In today's world, inclusive leadership has become both a timely and a timeless requirement for progress. From my experiences serving customers, generating growth and value for shareholders, collaborating with partners and suppliers, and managing diverse teams around the world, to my leadership roles in nonprofit governance and now in the corporate boardroom, I've learned that optimizing for success has always required looking at the bigger picture and applying the insights to my own leadership practice.

But consider the promise of bigger leadership: a shift, already in motion, that can have a real impact on society. When we each tap into diverse groups of people and communities to broaden our talent pools, we create greater progress, catalyzing more innovation and higher productivity. When we treat every person with respect, civility, and grace, we can focus our energy on creative enterprises, elevating our everyday lives. And is it too ambitious to suggest that bigger leadership can lift many from poverty and close the gaps in our education and healthcare systems while countering climate change? I believe it's possible. The mechanisms are available to us, like levers we can pull if we make the choice to work together.

To recap, what do these bigger leaders do? What do they create that is different from others? They develop inclusive cultures characterized by:

- **Work** that is guided by an inspiring purpose. The organization clearly embodies their core and aspirational values, and bigger leaders model these around the clock and under duress. Ever mindful of their stakeholders, they deeply understand how performance is prioritized. This understanding is embedded in their operating model and measurements.

- An engaged, diverse **workforce**, performing at optimum potential. This is done with a keen focus on their humanity as complex individuals, caring for their well-being, and infusing their career contributions with vitality. Every member of the team feels comfortable with their authenticity as they're supported by a true culture of belonging.

- A trusted, safe, and flexible **workplace** where each person can contribute their best no matter where, when, and how. This includes workspaces that spark meaningful connection, engagement, collaboration, and innovation. These organizational models support employees, not only in their current job, but in their careers and lives. These types of work environments also enable greater success because they are more resilient and adaptable.

Sometimes you may have felt overwhelmed while reading this book. But the opportunities ahead, including the betterment of our world, are greater than the challenges. Bigger leaders hold the key. Having led and supported customers around the globe from the front lines, from the C-suite, and now from the boardroom, I can confidently say that today's rapidly evolving world demands inclusion as a core leadership competency. For generations we have been required to think bigger—it is now time to lead bigger.

Remember that building organizations and cultures from a place of caring can be some of the most fulfilling work you do in your lifetime. Helping those around us to discover their unique value and purpose, and watching them succeed? Priceless.

The world demands bigger leaders, as they are the ones who bridge the gap in the workplace and help us see the possibilities within ourselves and others, pushing us to look outside our inner kaleidoscopes. And they do so in ways that connect, not divide, us.

I hope to meet you along the way as we forge the path together to becoming the bigger leaders the world needs now.

A FINAL MESSAGE

Dear Reader,

Thank you for your interest in this book and for giving me an opportunity to engage with you. I've always believed that leadership is a choice that transcends title, tenure, and time as well as any one aspect of our identity. Leadership can help us all, but it must evolve along with the times.

Every one of us has the power to lead bigger. If we work together, we will make a greater difference not only in each of our roles, but for all those around us and society as a whole.

My hope is that you will choose to lead bigger in all facets of your life. Your gifts and contributions are so needed in the world today if we are to create a future that's bigger (and brighter) than anything we could've dreamed.

In Gratitude,

ACKNOWLEDGMENTS

Little did I know that when I started a weekly blog to my team back in the fall of 2010 my inner writer would be sparked. My initial purpose for blogging was to better connect with my people, who were scattered around the country and eventually around the world as my roles evolved. As time went on, it became clear to me that there was so much that one could do by using the written word. Connection is a given, but sharing my thoughts in a timely and authentic way provided me with bountiful opportunities for making a difference in people's lives. By writing, I felt I could provide hope, insights, different perspectives, lessons learned, and more, to ultimately help and support others. The feedback I received from AT&T employees was tremendous and fueled me to develop this skill, eventually aspiring to write a book of my own someday.

After countless hours of hard work, a wide array of emotions, and incredible support from many, I find that someday is today.

Thank you to my literary agent, Scott Miller, and the team (Tony Di Constanzo, Ireland Duvall) at Gray + Miller Agency, for believing in my idea from the beginning and helping me take the first steps forward (while prodding me along the way).

To Stephen M. R. Covey, thank you for encouraging my early dreams of becoming a thought leader. Your words of wisdom on the importance of writing a book because of my unique perspective helped me believe I could actually do it, just because you said so.

To Meg Hackett, who has been on this book journey with me since the beginning, *thank you* does not sufficiently capture my appreciation for you. From the proposal on, without you, I'd literally be nowhere. I could not have asked for a better partner in this process and am eternally grateful for you. Your skills, insights, and talents (especially patience!) abound, and I'm the lucky one to have been able to partner with you over the years. To Nicole Volpe Miller, thank you for saying yes to join Meg and me in this ambitious endeavor. Your contributions and journalistic flair have helped shape this work into what we know to be an even more compelling timely and timeless conversation about inclusion. To Nereo Zago, thank you for saying yes to being my "graphics guy." Your keen creative eye has been vital to bringing my visualizations to life in simple, compelling illustrations. To Laney Hawes, thank you for lending your permissions prowess to this work and keeping our work on the straight and narrow.

To General Stanley McChrystal, Arianna Huffington, and Adam Grant, thank you for lending your thoughts to this work. Your insights continue to inspire leaders of all kinds, including and especially me.

To my AT&T clan, thank you. Thousands and thousands of colleagues and comrades around the world connected by the power of purpose. I'm so proud of what we accomplished together over the course of more than three decades—serving customers and innovating for growth while helping to transform the world. Together, we took on our role as stewards of the essential services we provided to businesses and consumers alike. While we were not perfect, as no business or human is, we were committed to doing the right thing, building trust, and learning always. Working with you, our customers, partners, and stakeholders created the seeds of leading bigger, and I'm grateful for the experiences we've shared.

To the entire #Tsisterhood, which lasts long past employment, especially Cynt Marshall, Joan Marsh, and Joni Arison, I'm forever grateful for your friendship. To Belinda Rodriguez, Marvy Moore, and Corey Anthony, thanks for saying yes to our Women of Color initiative. Together we made a huge difference for hundreds of women and their supporters. To the original founders and ongoing members of AT&T Women of Business and the Asia Pacific Women's Network (special thanks to Mary Beth Asher, Trish Renz, and Pamela Osborne), each one of you is a fabulous and fierce leader. Don't ever forget that together, we're unstoppable.

Khal Sukkar, you helped shape the earliest notions I had of becoming a writer. Through three years of your generosity in the employee auction, I benefited in person from your encouragement—telling me that I could, should, and must write a book someday.

To my 4A→APCA→InspirAsian family, yeah, I know I said that we shouldn't use *family* to describe work—but you are the exception. Together over the years, we bonded over good food, good times, and good work—to support our community as we shared in unity, our pride for our culture, histories, and peoples. To my teams across the business from Select Accounts & Indirect Channels, Premier Client Group, National Business, Integrator Solutions, and AT&T Business as a whole, thank you. Such meaningful relationships were made both inside and outside of the company through such shared experiences and growth—whether it was #SelltoExcel, #ReadySetGrow, #GoforGrowth, #PCGPeeps4ever, #NationalBizNation, and more. Thank you also to the world's best global events team, led by Karen Carroll (aka dahling PP roomie), whose approach to customer and employee experiences was always top-notch. You were all integral to enabling bigger leadership for me and my team throughout my entire career.

To every one of my leadership teams in the roles I've had over the decades, thank you. It was an honor to serve you and collaborate together across our beloved company. I'm grateful for your contributions and for the ways you each helped both me and our business grow. To my most formative, dare I say, top three bosses, thank you for showing me in my early years what leading bigger looked like. I credit your leadership with some of the most critical learnings I had in my career. Of my twenty-six bosses: number one, Sandy Hall; number four, Pat Traynor; and number six, Glenn Swift. To every single one of my managers, I learned something from each of you, and for that I'm thankful.

No leader can get the job done without the right team of people around them, enabling and supporting them. There's no question that my leadership journey was made possible by the choice of people around me, especially those who boldly accepted the assignment of chief of staff: Brian Blount (thanks for saying yes twice!), Chris Donan (thanks for *really* wanting the job), Blake Haydon, Ania Wolecka-Jernigan, Chris Hollmer, Larry Perez, and Alvaro Medieros, to name a few. And as anyone who has to manage a calendar knows, the administrative excellence around you is key to your success—thank you to Daria Hill, Pat McKenna, Deldee Castorena, Ina McGhee-Merritt, and Tracy Harris. What incredible years we shared. And to Cathy Paprzycki, who helped me with blogs and decades of communications to my people, thank you for helping me amplify and refine my voice. All of you are the most amazing of people and truly bigger leaders in your own right.

I'm often asked what I'm most proud of during my tenure at AT&T. The answer is easy—it was during the last of my assignments at the company, as CEO of AT&T Business. The work we did throughout the pandemic and emergence out of it was truly a model of trust, purpose, and performance. From supporting our people to supporting diverse customers around the world across all industries to delivering innovative solutions for our first responders, we had a profound impact. We helped keep the world moving forward. Shout-out to my entire leadership team! You led bigger—with unmatched intensity and dedication. What an honor it was to lead with you. Special thanks also to my AT&T Business staff and support team, without whom, I literally could not have done my job: Brian, Cathy and Tracy, Trey Winter, Jessica Bourne, Jonathan Biggs, Kally Masino, Stephanie Matthews, Tingting Chou, Tony Mazarani, Laurie Shults, Kelly Barr, Mike Labunski, Joe Moore, Jason Jones, Jonathan Drexel, and Tim Raymond. And to my partner teams across PR, Legal, CFO, and HR, you are best in class, and it was an honor to serve alongside you. Thank you for making us (including me) better: Rick Gomez, Stephen Stokes, Alexis Aziz, Anne Tidrick, Pete Schaffer, and Darryl Guy. Many of the initiatives covered in this book, such as Connection Circles and Candid Conversations, would have never become a reality without you. All of you showed me what the power of bigger can do.

To those early leaders across the APIA community, especially Bill Imada and Karen Narasaki, you helped reveal a greater purpose to me back in the 2000s—the power of connection, the power of equity, and the power of using a platform for good. The kernels of leading bigger across our community outside of AT&T began with my relationships with you and your teams. Special thanks to all associated with APIA Scholars (formerly known as APIASF), Advancing Justice—Asian American Justice Center, especially my now lifelong friends, Wai-Ling Eng and Jacinta Titiali'i-Abbott, with whom my community journey continues to be greatly enriched. To our friend Michael Fung, you were an early trailblazer for all of us and are missed every day. Thank you for being an amazing role model and friend.

To my DFW group of Asian leaders and allies across AAEN, the Orchid Giving Circle, Asian Chamber of Texas, and more, your commitment to making an impact both for your businesses and for our community is inspiring. I'm proud to work alongside you as we make even more progress together.

To Helen Chang and Bella Malick, you are both brilliant and beautiful people! Thank you for supporting me in the creation of my brand, initial website, and more.

To my Boston, NJ, and Boxing BFFs, Judy Hedman, Lisa Waddell, Cara Hegadorn, Sheila Price, Hope Nguyen Shen, thank you for your friendship, which is present with me every day, even though we may be miles apart. An integral part of leading bigger is the care for those around you. Your support for me has been unwavering, and as fellow moms, you've shown me throughout the years that motherhood is in fact the biggest (and most important) job ever. You are all role models. Love you!

To the OG team at FranklinCovey who invited me to be part of *The Leader's Guide to Unconscious Bias: How to Reframe Bias, Cultivate Connection, and Create High-Performing Teams*, thank you. The work with you on this book showed me what could be possible, and it was an honor to collaborate with you. Shout-out to Pamela Fuller, Mark Murphy, of course—Meg, Scott, Annie Oswald, Deb Lund, Zach Kristensen, Bob Whitman, Paul Walker, and more.

To my insightful and talented editor and assistant editor at Simon & Schuster, Stephanie Frerich and Brittany Adames, thank you for betting on me and for your unwavering support of this project. From the beginning of this effort, you believed in my conviction that I had something important and different to say—and your encouragement, direction, and feedback have been invaluable. I extend my gratitude to the entire publishing and editing team involved, especially Jonathan Karp, CEO; Irene Kheradi, associate publisher; Priscilla Painton, editor in chief; and the skilled team of professionals across the organization: Tyanni Niles, Cat Boyd, Amanda Mulholland, Lauren Gomez, Zoe Kaplan, Phil Metcalf, Meryll Preposi, Beth Maglione, Samantha Cohen, Mikaela Bielawski, Wendy Blum, Rick Willett, Nancy Inglis, Martha Kennedy, Emma Shaw, Natalia Olbinski, Tom Spain, Ray Chokov, Nicole Moran, Michale Nardullo, Mabel Taveras, Lyndsay Brueggemann, Winona Lukito, Cat Boyd, Tyanni Niles, and Carolyn Levin. All of you brought this book to life, literally. Thank you for your contributions to it.

To my beta readers and those who graciously gave their attention and time to read drafts, give feedback on cover designs, and more, thank you. Your encouragement, enthusiasm, and interest kept me going.

To Liz Wiseman, my "book buddy" multiplier, thank you for being so willing to show me the ropes. To Mark Fortier and his team at Fortier PR as well as Ken Gillett and his team at Target Marketing Digital, I could not have asked for better partners to launch my first solo book.

I've dedicated this book to my parents, Dr. Ming-Chwan and Joann Chao-Chu Chow. It is they who instilled in me the belief that your life's purpose was to be good, do good, for good. Their bold decision to leave their native country of Taiwan in pursuit of a bigger and better life set forth a path for our family that serves as the foundation of this work. They are my ultimate role models, as their courage, compassion, intelligence, and dedication to others are constant reminders for me to strive to make a difference, always.

To my husband, Bob (aka Bob from Accounting, IT, Transportation, Construction, Security, etc), you have and will forever be the most important enabler to my ability to lead bigger. It is only because you have been so supportive of my career from the very beginning of our marriage, willingly leaving the workforce early, even when it was not common or popular for men to do so. Your love, support, and impeccable ability to get things done (albeit sometimes slowly, LOL) have kept us and our family moving forward. We are the yang to each other's yin. Thank you for embarking on our journey of life together so many years ago. LYH.

To my little brother, Danny, the other OG member of the "Chow Dynasty," I'm honored to be your big sister (the best sister in the world, in fact). So proud of how you lead bigger in your profession as an ob-gyn, helping so many families in so many ways across the generations.

To my daughters, Alana and Camryn, you are the light in my life. You are my reason for being, the source of my inspiration, and the most precious gift from God. You are also my greatest legacy. Being your mom is the best and most important job I've ever had. I'm so proud of the young women you've become. To you and all the women of your generation and those to follow, as well as anyone of any generation who has felt they could not become the leader they aspired to be, *believe in bigger*. You can dream anything, create anything, be anything, and do anything. Your greatest superpower is *you*.

To everyone who has joined me on this journey even if your name is not mentioned here, know that I'm grateful for your support and our connection.

Finally, to all of my readers, whether you are a leader today or an aspiring leader of tomorrow, this book and the opportunity to lead bigger are now in your hands.

NOTES

CHAPTER 1: THE OPPORTUNITY TO LEAD BIGGER

9 *According to the* Harvard Business Review: Wei Zheng, Jennifer Kim, Ronit Kark, and Lisa Mascolo, "What Makes an Inclusive Leader?," *Harvard Business Review*, September 27, 2023, https://hbr.org/2023/09/what-makes-an-inclusive-leader.

CHAPTER 2: PURPOSE: BEYOND THE DAILY GRIND

22 *Gallup found that:* Vibhas Ratanjee and Ed O'Boyle, "Diagnosing a Broken Culture—and What to Do About It," Gallup.com Workplace, August 4, 2023, https://www.gallup.com/workplace/509069/diagnosing-broken-culture.aspx.

23 *According to Deloitte Global Gen Z and Millennial Survey:* Elizabeth Faber, "Millennial and Gen Z Employees Are Rejecting Assignments, Turning Down Offers, and Seeking Purpose. Here's What They Expect of Their Employers, According to Deloitte's Latest Survey," *Fortune*, July 6, 2023, https://fortune.com/2023/07/06/millennial-gen-z-employees-are-rejecting-assignments-turning-down-offers-and-seeking-purpose-they-expect-of-employers-according-to-deloittes-latest-survey/.

23 *Fifty percent of Gen Z:* Kim Parker and Ruth Igielnik, "On the Cusp of Adulthood and Facing an Uncertain Future: What We Know About Gen Z So Far," Pew Research Center, May 14, 2020, https://www.pewresearch.org/social-trends/2020/05/14/on-the-cusp-of-adulthood-and-facing-an-uncertain-future-what-we-know-about-gen-z-so-far-2/.

23 *20 percent identify:* Jeffrey M. Jones, "LGBT Identification in U.S. Ticks Up to 7.1%," Gallup.com Politics, February 17, 2022, https://news.gallup.com/poll/389792/lgbt-identification-ticks-up.aspx.

25 *Imagine my surprise:* Philippe Rothlin and Peter Werder, *Diagnose Boreout* (Redline Wirtschaft, 2007).

28 *The e-bike market is predicted:* "Electric Bike Market Size, Share, & COVID-19 Impact Analysis," Fortune Business Insights, May 2023, https://www.fortunebusinessinsights.com/electric-e-bike-market-102022; and David Zipper, "How E-Bike Rebates Will Make Cycling Safer," Bloomberg.com,

February 9, 2023, https://www.bloomberg.com/news/articles/2023-02-09/denver-s-e-bike-rebate-program-has-a-hidden-power.

35 *In this way:* Whitney Dailey, "Leading with Purpose: The New Business Norm?," *Stanford Social Innovation Review,* August 15, 2018, https://ssir.org/articles/entry/leading_with_purpose_the_new_business_norm.

38 *Lululemon put out a statement:* Curtis Bunn, "Lululemon Founder's Remarks Have Some DEI Experts Calling for Boycotts to Combat 'Regressive Values,'" NBC News, January 6, 2024, https://www.nbcnews.com/news/nbcblk/lululemon-chip-wilson-dei-boycott-rcna132338.

CHAPTER 3: VALUES: ALIGN PRINCIPLES WITH BEHAVIOR

46 *"planning to leave their company":* EYAmericas, "2022 EY US Generation Survey Reveals Impact Company Culture Plays in Employee Retention," press release, October 13, 2022, https://www.ey.com/en_us/news/2022/10/ey-generation-survey-reveals-impact-company-culture-plays-in-employee-retention.

46 *Gen Z increasingly expects:* EY.com, "Gen Z Activism," https://www.ey.com/en_us/consulting/is-gen-z-the-spark-we-need-to-see-the-light-report/gen-z-activism.

46 *Twenty percent of Gen Alpha:* beanodigital, "Gen Alpha Mini Heroes," Beano Brain, July 18, 2023, https://www.beanobrain.com/post/mini-gen-alpha-mini-heroes.

46 *Research shows that values alignment:* Paul Ingram and Yoonjin Choi, "What Does Your Company Really Stand For?" *Harvard Business Review,* November–December 2022, hbr.org, https://hbr.org/2022/11/what-does-your-company-really-stand-for.

49 *characterized by toxic behaviors:* SHRM Foundation, "SHRM Reports Toxic Workplace Cultures Cost Billions," September 25, 2019, https://www.shrm.org/about/press-room/shrm-reports-toxic-workplace-cultures-cost-billions.

51 *All too often leaders assume:* Ingram and Choi, "What Does Your Company Really Stand For?"

CHAPTER 4: PERFORMANCE: DELIVER RESULTS *AND* IMPACT

61 *Ships were waiting:* Jiaguo Liu, Xinrui Wang, and Jihong Chen, "Port Congestion Under the COVID-19 Pandemic: The Simulation-Based Countermeasures," *Computers & Industrial Engineering* 183 (2023): 109474, doi: 10.1016/j.cie.2023.109474.

68 *Later, as researchers worked:* Tom Simonite, "To Compete with Google, OpenAI Seeks Investors—and Profits," *Wired,* March 12, 2019, https://www.wired.com/story/compete-google-openai-seeks-investorsand-profits/; Aaron Mok, "ChatGPT Could Cost over $700,000 per Day to Operate. Microsoft Is Reportedly

Trying to Make It Cheaper," Business Insider, https://www.businessinsider
.com/how-much-chatgpt-costs-openai-to-run-estimate-report-2023-4.

CHAPTER 5: WELL-BEING: ELEVATE PERFORMANCE THROUGH CARE AND BELONGING

76 *The U.S. surgeon general reports:* "The U.S. Surgeon General's Framework
for Workplace Mental Health & Well-Being," Current Priorities of the U.S.
Surgeon General, 2022, https://www.hhs.gov/surgeongeneral/priorities
/workplace-well-being/index.html.

76 *McKinsey research found:* McKinsey Health Institute, "Present Company
Included: Prioritizing Mental Health and Well-Being for All," McKinsey
.com, October 10, 2022, https://www.mckinsey.com/mhi/our-insights
/present-company-included-prioritizing-mental-health-and-well-being
-for-all.

77 *A third of workers:* The Hartford News, "The Hartford's New Study Finds
Employers Believe Worsening Employee Mental Health Is Hurting Their
Financial Performance," press release, April 25, 2022, https://newsroom.the
hartford.com/newsroom-home/news-releases/news-releases-details/2022
/The-Hartfords-New-Study-Finds-Employers-Believe-Worsening-Employee
-Mental-Health-Is-Hurting-Their-Financial-Performance/default.aspx.

77 *The findings from McKinsey's global survey:* McKinsey Health Institute, "Present
Company Included: Prioritizing Mental Health and Well-Being for All."

77 *because 84 percent of workers say:* "The U.S. Surgeon General's Framework
for Workplace Mental Health & Well-Being."

77 *According to SHRM:* Jennifer Moss, "Dealing with Social Isolation," SHRM,
April 25, 2020, https://www.shrm.org/topics-tools/news/all-things-work
/dealing-social-isolation.

78 *Gen Z has higher rates of anxiety:* Niki Jorgensen, "Council Post: How to Support
Gen-Z Employees' Mental Health at Work," *Forbes,* May 16, 2023, https://www
.forbes.com/sites/forbeshumanresourcescouncil/2023/05/16/how-to-support
-gen-z-employees-mental-health-at-work/.

78 *Gen X is shouldering intense caregiving:* Alex Gailey, "More Than Half of Americans Say Money Negatively Impacts Their Mental Health," Bankrate, May 8,
2023, https://www.bankrate.com/personal-finance/financial-wellness-survey/.

78 *Clearly a single approach:* McKinsey Health Institute, "Present Company
Included: Prioritizing Mental Health and Well-Being for All."

80 *People who live in rural communities:* Dawn A. Morales, Crystal L. Barksdale,
and Andrea C. Beckel-Mitchener, "A Call to Action to Address Rural Mental
Health Disparities," *Journal of Clinical and Translational Science* 4, no. 5 (2020):
463–467, doi: 10.1017/cts.2020.42.

80 *Country-specific cultural nuances:* McKinsey Health Institute, "Present Company Included: Prioritizing Mental Health and Well-Being for All."

81 *But almost 70 percent of people:* Zuva Seven, "How Do Other Countries Deal with Mental Health?" Verywell Mind, July 5, 2023, https://www.verywellmind.com/how-do-other-countries-deal-with-mental-health-7556304.

81 *While 30 percent of the U.S. workforce:* "The Hartford's New Research: Race and Culture Affect U.S. Workers' Comfort Talking About Mental Health," The Hartford News, July 14, 2022, https://newsroom.thehartford.com/newsroom-home/news-releases/news-releases-details/2022/The-Hartfords-New-Research-Race-and-Culture-Affect-U.S.-Workers-Comfort-Talking-About-Mental-Health/default.aspx.

81 *The LGBTQ+ community is two and a half times:* Chris Michalak and Marlette Jackson, "Supporting the Well-Being of Your Underrepresented Employees," *Harvard Business Review,* March 4, 2022, https://hbr.org/2022/03/supporting-the-well-being-of-your-underrepresented-employees.

86 *Belonging is central to all humans:* Julia Taylor Kennedy and Pooja Jain-Link, "What Does It Take to Build a Culture of Belonging?" *Harvard Business Review,* June 21, 2021, https://hbr.org/2021/06/what-does-it-take-to-build-a-culture-of-belonging.

87 *Perhaps surprisingly:* "EY Belonging Barometer Workplace Study," https://www.ey.com/en_us/diversity-inclusiveness/ey-belonging-barometer-workplace-study.

89 *Let's look at a set of experiments:* "The Value of Belonging at Work: The Business Case for Investing in Workplace Inclusion," March 12, 2024, https://grow.betterup.com/resources/the-value-of-belonging-at-work-the-business-case-for-investing-in-workplace-inclusion/watch.

90 *Research has demonstrated that fostering belonging:* Colleen Bordeaux, Betsy Grace, and Naina Sabherwal, "Elevating the Workforce Experience: The Belonging Relationship," Deloitte, November 23, 2021, https://www2.deloitte.com/us/en/blog/human-capital-blog/2021/what-is-belonging-in-the-workplace.html.

90 *The American Psychological Association has found:* American Psychological Association, "2023 Work in America Survey: Workplaces as Engines of Psychological Health and Well-Being," https://www.apa.org/pubs/reports/work-in-america/2023-workplace-health-well-being.

90 *The "belonging scores" below:* Coqual, "The Power of Belonging," https://coqual.org/reports/the-power-of-belonging/.

96 *Workers often report:* Karyn Twaronite, "Five Findings on the Importance of Belonging," EY, May 11, 2019, https://www.ey.com/en_us/diversity-inclusiveness/ey-belonging-barometer-workplace-study.

97 *One in five Americans:* Catalyst, "Women of Color in the United States (Quick

Take)," February 1, 2023, https://www.catalyst.org/research/women-of-color
-in-the-united-states/.

97 *Importantly, women of color:* Emily Field et al., "Women in the Workplace
2023 Report," McKinsey, October 4, 2023, https://www.mckinsey.com/featured
-insights/diversity-and-inclusion/women-in-the-workplace.

98 *My concerns were backed up:* Alexis Krivkovich et al., "Women in the Workplace
2017," McKinsey & Company, October 2017, https://womenintheworkplace
.com/2017.

SPECIAL SEGMENT: DEMYSTIFYING UNCONSCIOUS BIAS: BEAUTY BIAS AND LOOKISM

104 *We gather up to 80 percent:* Barbara Koltuska-Haskin, "How Colors Affect Brain
Functioning," *Psychology Today,* January 29, 2023, https://www.psychologytoday
.com/us/blog/how-my-brain-works/202301/how-colors-affect-brain-functioning.

105 *For instance, in certain communities in Asia:* Isabel M. Scott et al., "Human
Preferences for Sexually Dimorphic Faces May Be Evolutionarily Novel,"
Proceedings of the National Academy of Sciences of the United States of America
111, no. 40 (2014): 14388–93, doi: 10.1073/pnas.1409643111.

106 *and in Namibia:* Piotr Sorokowski, Agnieszka Sorokowska, and Mara Mber-
ira, "Are Preferences for Legs Length Universal? Data from a Semi-Nomadic
Himba Population from Namibia," *Journal of Social Psychology* 152, no. 3
(2012): 370–78, doi: 10.1080/00224545.2011.609845.

106 *Less attractive people are less likely:* Tomas Chamorro-Premuzic, "Attractive People Get Unfair Advantages at Work. AI Can Help," *Harvard Business
Review,* October 31, 2019, https://hbr.org/2019/10/attractive-people-get-unfair
-advantages-at-work-ai-can-help.

106 *Attractive people are thought:* Chamorro-Premuzic, "Attractive People Get
Unfair Advantages at Work. AI Can Help."

106 *Malcolm Gladwell famously revealed:* Malcolm Gladwell, *Blink: The Power of
Thinking Without Thinking* (New York: Back Bay Books, 2007).

106 *Smaller-statured women:* Aysha Imtiaxz, "Height Discrimination: How 'Heightism' Affects Careers," BBC, August 26, 2022, https://www.bbc.com/worklife
/article/20220825-height-discrimination-how-heightism-affects-careers.

107 *Women are much more susceptible:* Euna Han, Edward C. Norton, and Lisa M.
Powell, "Direct and Indirect Effects of Body Weight on Adult Wages," *Economics and Human Biology* 9, no. 4 (2011): 381–92, doi: 10.1016/j.ehb.2011.07.002.

107 *Body inclusivity is:* Jennifer "Jay" Palumbro, "The Body Positive Movement
Encourages Inclusion, Not Obesity," *Forbes,* May 12, 2022, https://www
.forbes.com/sites/jenniferpalumbo/2022/05/12/how-the-body-positive-move
ment-doesnt-encourage-obesity-but-inclusion/.

108 *One of the reasons why:* Ruchika Tulshyan, "Return to Office? Some Women of Color Aren't Ready," *New York Times,* June 23, 2021, https://www.nytimes.com/2021/06/23/us/return-to-office-anxiety.html.

108 *The wearing of masks also:* Matthew Rozsa, "Wearing Face Masks Erases 'Beauty Bias,' Study Finds," *Salon,* December 21, 2021, https://www.salon.com/2021/12/21/wearing-face-masks-erases-beauty-bias-study-finds/.

108 *For decades, Black women:* Jihan Forbes, "How the Pandemic Refocused Black Women's Commitment to Their Wellness," *Allure,* May 3, 2021, https://www.allure.com/sponsored/story/aarp-2021-survey-black-women-pandemic-beauty-wellness-habits.

CHAPTER 6: DIMENSIONALITY: EXPAND YOUR UNDERSTANDING OF PEOPLE

111 *She coined it in a legal context:* Kimberlé Crenshaw, "Demarginalizing the Intersection of Race and Sex: A Black Feminist Critique of Antidiscrimination Doctrine, Feminist Theory and Antiracist Politics," *University of Chicago Legal Forum* 140 (1989), 139–67.

111 *Reflecting more than two decades later:* "Kimberlé Crenshaw on Intersectionality, More Than Two Decades Later," News from Columbia Law, June 8, 2017, https://www.law.columbia.edu/news/archive/kimberle-crenshaw-intersectionality-more-two-decades-later.

114 *Gen Zers generally believe:* Kim Parker, Nikki Graf, and Ruth Igielnik, "Generation Z Looks a Lot Like Millennials on Key Social and Political Issues," Pew Research Center's Social & Demographic Trends Project (blog), January 17, 2019, https://www.pewresearch.org/social-trends/2019/01/17/generation-z-looks-a-lot-like-millennials-on-key-social-and-political-issues/.

115 *Beginning in 2024:* Mitra Toossi, "Labor Force Projections to 2024: The Labor Force Is Growing, but Slowly," *Monthly Labor Review,* U.S. Bureau of Labor Statistics, December 2015, https://www.bls.gov/opub/mlr/2015/article/labor-force-projections-to-2024.htm#:~:text=The%20U.S.%20labor%20force—the,reach%20163.8%20million%20in%202024.&text=The%20labor%20force%20is%20anticipated,over%20the%202014–24%20period.

115 *People aged fifty-five and older:* Megan W. Gerhardt, Josephine Nachemson-Ekwall, and Brandon Fogel, "Harnessing the Power of Age Diversity," *Harvard Business Review,* March 8, 2022, https://hbr.org/2022/03/harnessing-the-power-of-age-diversity.

115 *Boomers did as much:* Gerhardt, Nachemson-Ekwall, and Fogel, "Harnessing the Power of Age Diversity."

117 *As the* Harvard Business Review *puts it:* Gerhardt, Nachemson-Ekwall, and Fogel, "Harnessing the Power of Age Diversity."

118 *For example, just the sight of an Asian face:* Yi Zheng and Arthur G. Samuel, "Does Seeing an Asian Face Make Speech Sound More Accented?" *Attention, Perception, & Psychophysics* 79, no. 6 (2017): 1841–59, doi: 10.3758/s13414-017-1329-2.

118 *Despite the fact that non-native speakers:* Billy Morgan, "How Your Speech Could Impact Your Salary," University of Chicago News, November 6, 2019, https://news .uchicago.edu/story/how-your-speech-could-impact-your-salary.

118 *According to the BBC:* Christine Ro, "The Pervasive Problem of 'Linguistic Racism,'" June 3, 2021, https://www.bbc.com/worklife/article/20210528-the -pervasive-problem-of-linguistic-racism.

118 *"In Japan, the Tōhoku regional accent":* Sarah Todd, "Have a Strong Accent? Here's How That Hurts Your Paycheck," *Quartz,* February 8, 2020, https://qz.com /work/1797510/why-workers-with-regional-accents-make-less-money.

119 *But as with all negative biases:* Ro, "The Pervasive Problem of 'Linguistic Racism.'"

120 *According to HubSpot:* Leslie Ye, "How to Be in Sales as an Introvert," August 7, 2023, https://blog.hubspot.com/sales/are-extroverts-or-introverts-better-sales people.

120 *"Whereas just 50% of the general population":* Adam Grant, Francesca Gino, and David A. Hofmann, "The Hidden Advantages of Quiet Bosses," *Harvard Business Review,* December 1, 2010, https://hbr.org/2010/12/the-hidden -advantages-of-quiet-bosses.

120 *Introverted CEOs exceeded:* Jena McGregor, "Introverts Tend to Be Better CEOs—and Other Surprising Traits of Top-Performing Executives," *Washington Post,* April 17, 2017, https://www.washingtonpost.com/news/on-leadership /wp/2017/04/17/introverts-tend-to-be-better-ceos-and-other-surprising-traits -of-top-performing-executives/.

120 *Overall, one in seven people:* Allaya Cooks-Campbell, "Unlock Creativity by Making Space for Neurodiversity in the Workplace," BetterUP, June 24, 2022, https://www.betterup.com/blog/neurodiversity-in-the-workplace.

121 *Half of UK managers:* Ludmila Praslova, "Neurodivergent People Make Great Leaders, Not Just Employees," *Fast Company,* December 15, 2021, https:// www.fastcompany.com/90706149/neurodivergent-people-make-great-leaders -not-just-employees.

121 *"The unemployment rate of autistic college":* Praslova, "Neurodivergent People Make Great Leaders, Not Just Employees."

121 *JPMorgan Chase found that:* Hayleigh Colombo, "How JP Morgan's Autism at Work Program Is Breaking Boundaries for Neurodiverse Workers," Columbus Business First, May 10, 2021, https://www.bizjournals.com/columbus /news/2021/04/14/jpmorgan-chase-autism-at-work-program.html.

122 *About a third of people in the United States:* Marguerite Ward, "The Equity Talk: Muslim Women Say Their Voices Aren't Heard in the Workplace. That's a

Massive Problem Corporate Execs Need to Address," Business Insider, July 11, 2022, https://www.businessinsider.com/equity-talk-muslim-women-voices -arent-heard-religion-faith-workplace-2022-4.

124 *Research conducted by the Society:* "SHRM Announces Program to De-Polarize Workplaces, Offer Businesses Unifying Alternative to Mainstream Diversity Practices," SHRM, May 9, 2022, https://www.shrm.org/about/press-room /shrm-announces-program-to-de-polarize-workplaces-offer-businesses -unifying-alternative-to-mainstream-diversity-practices.

124 *And 44 percent of employees:* Chloe Taylor, "Workers Are Avoiding Their Colleagues Because of Conflicting Political Views—and Employers Are Afraid to Choose Sides, HR Expert Says," *Fortune,* July 7, 2022, https://fortune .com/2022/07/27/workers-avoiding-colleagues-conflicting-political-views -employers-afraid-choose-sides-gartner/.

124 *According to the Cato Institute:* Emily Elkins, "62% of Americans Say They Have Political Views They're Afraid to Share," July 22, 2020, https://www.cato .org/survey-reports/poll-62-americans-say-they-have-political-views-theyre -afraid-share#32-worry-their-political-views-could-harm-their-employment.

124 *Younger people and more educated:* Elkins, "62% of Americans Say They Have Political Views They're Afraid to Share."

126 *But as much as we fear:* Feng Shi, Misha Teplitskiy, Eamon Duede, and James A. Evans, "The Wisdom of Polarized Crowds," *Nature Human Behaviour* 3, no. 4 (2019): 329–36, doi: 10.1038/s41562-019-0541-6.

127 *Researchers also explain:* Feng Shi, Feng, Misha Teplitskiy, Eamon Duede, and James A. Evans, "Are Politically Diverse Teams More Effective?" *Harvard Business Review,* July 15, 2019, https://hbr.org/2019/07/are-politically -diverse-teams-more-effective.

127 *Over one-third of Gen Z:* Anna Brown, "About 5% of Young Adults in the U.S. Say Their Gender Is Different from Their Sex Assigned at Birth," June 7, 2022, Pew Research Center (blog), https://www.pewresearch.org/short -reads/2022/06/07/about-5-of-young-adults-in-the-u-s-say-their-gender-is -different-from-their-sex-assigned-at-birth/.

127 *Nearly 60 percent of Gen Z:* Nikki Graf, "About Four-in-Ten U.S. Adults Say Forms Should Offer More than Two Gender Options," Pew Research Center (blog), December 18, 2019, https://www.pewresearch.org/short -reads/2019/12/18/gender-options-on-forms-or-online-profiles/.

127 *Globally, 25 percent of Gen Z:* Lisa Kenney, "Companies Can't Ignore Shifting Gender Norms," *Harvard Business Review,* April 8, 2020, https://hbr.org/2020/04 /companies-cant-ignore-shifting-gender-norms.

127 *Adults under thirty:* Anna Brown, "About 5% of Young Adults in the U.S. Say Their Gender Is Different from Their Sex Assigned at Birth," Pew Research Center (blog), https://www.pewresearch.org/short-reads/2022/06/07/about-5-of-young

-adults-in-the-u-s-say-their-gender-is-different-from-their-sex-assigned
-at-birth/.

127 *Although the percentage of transgender adults:* Anna Brown, "About 5%
of Young Adults in the U.S. Say Their Gender Is Different from Their Sex
Assigned at Birth."

128 *Pew Research currently finds:* Rachel Minkin and Anna Brown, "Rising Shares
of U.S. Adults Know Someone Who Is Transgender or Goes by Gender-
Neutral Pronouns," Pew Research Center (blog), July 27, 2021, https://www
.pewresearch.org/short-reads/2021/07/27/rising-shares-of-u-s-adults-know
-someone-who-is-transgender-or-goes-by-gender-neutral-pronouns/.

128 *Veterans represent just over:* "Employment Situation of Veterans Summary,"
U.S. Bureau of Labor Statistics, March 21, 2023, https://www.bls.gov/news
.release/vet.nro.htm.

128 *although they are more:* "Attracting Veterans to Your Workplace," SHRM,
https://www.shrm.org/topics-tools/tools/forms/attracting-veterans-to-work
place.

128 *Upwards of 20 percent of veterans:* Daniel H. Gillison Jr., "Veteran Mental
Health: Not All Wounds Are Visible," National Alliance on Mental Illness,
November 10, 2021, https://www.nami.org/Blogs/From-the-CEO/November
-2021/Veteran-Mental-Health-Not-All-Wounds-are-Visible.

129 *About 59 percent of employers:* "Attracting Veterans to Your Workplace,"
SHRM.

129 *Veterans face a stereotype:* "Research Shows Military Service Can Hurt Some
Job Seekers' Prospects," Duke, Fuqua School of Business, September 23, 2019,
https://www.fuqua.duke.edu/duke-fuqua-insights/how-military-service-can
-hurt-some-job-seekers%E2%80%99-prospects.

129 *Steve Cannon, CEO of AMB Group:* Liz Alton, "Understanding the Value
of Veterans in the Workplace at ADP's Inclusion Summit," ADP, November
2021, https://www.adp.com/spark/articles/2021/11/understanding-the-value
-of-veterans-in-the-workplace-at-adps-inclusion-summit.aspx.

CHAPTER 7: VITALITY: INVIGORATE THE EMPLOYEE EXPERIENCE

141 *In fact, 71 percent:* Jena McGregor, "Analysis: Nearly Three-Quarters of Executives Pick Proteges Who Look Just like Them," *Washington Post,* January 9,
2019, https://www.washingtonpost.com/business/2019/01/09/nearly-three
-quarters-executives-pick-proteges-who-look-just-like-them/.

143 *Every day, ten thousand baby boomers:* "United States," AARP International,
https://www.aarpinternational.org/initiatives/aging-readiness-competitive
ness-arc/united-states.

CHAPTER 8: SAFETY: CREATE AN ENVIRONMENT THAT FUELS CONTRIBUTION

153 *Harvard Business School professor:* "The Importance of Psychological Safety in the Workplace," McKinsey Quarterly Five Fifty, https://www.mckinsey.com /featured-insights/leadership/five-fifty-is-it-safe.

153 *As you might expect:* Amy C. Edmondson and Mark Mortensen, "What Psychological Safety Looks Like in a Hybrid Workplace," *Harvard Business Review,* April 19, 2021, https://hbr.org/2021/04/what-psychological-safety-looks-like -in-a-hybrid-workplace.

153 *As Laura Delizonna of Stanford University:* Laura Delizonna, "High-Performing Teams Need Psychological Safety: Here's How to Create It," *Harvard Business Review,* August 24, 2017, https://hbr.org/2017/08/high-performing -teams-need-psychological-safety-heres-how-to-create-it.

155 *Yet DDI's Global Leadership Forecast:* "Why Executives Need to Practice Vulnerable Leadership—and How to Do It," DDI, August 24, 2023, https://www .ddiworld.com/blog/vulnerable-leadership.

156 *According to McKinsey:* "What Is Psychological Safety?" McKinsey & Company, July 17, 2023, https://www.mckinsey.com/featured-insights/mckinsey-explainers /what-is-psychological-safety.

159 *employees with a growth mindset:* Qiang Liu and Yuqiong Tong, "Employee Growth Mindset and Innovative Behavior: The Roles of Employee Strengths Use and Strengths-Based Leadership," *Frontiers in Psychology* 13 (2022): 814154, doi: 10.3389/fpsyg.2022.814154.

159 *Such workplaces and bosses are poisonous:* Jane Thier, "American Workers Hate Their Jobs So Much That Nearly Half of Them Wouldn't Wish It on Their Worst Enemy," *Fortune,* November 15, 2022, https://fortune.com/2022/11/15 /american-workers-hate-their-jobs/.

160 *In China, such behavior is called* lying flat: Jack Kelly, "Workers in China Have Their Own Version of Quiet Quitting and Acting Your Wage: 'Huminerals' Are Extracted, Exploited and Disposed Of," *Forbes,* February 23, 2023, https://www.forbes.com /sites/jackkelly/2023/02/23/china-workers-have-their-version-of-quiet-quitting -and-acting-your-wage-huminerals-are-extracted-exploited-and-disposed-of/.

CHAPTER 9: BOUNDARIES: NAVIGATE PROFESSIONAL AND PERSONAL REALITIES

170 *After surveying 1,500 members:* "Report: Gen Z Finding Meaning," EY, https:// www.ey.com/en_us/consulting/is-gen-z-the-spark-we-need-to-see-the-light -report/gen-z-finding-meaning.

171 *According to BetterUp:* Madeline Miles, "Why Is Authenticity at Work So Hard?

5 Ways to Become More Authentic," BetterUp, March 14, 2022, https://www
.betterup.com/blog/authenticity-at-work.

172 *But only a tenth of employees:* Future Forum, "Future Forum Pulse Summer
Snapshot," July 2022, https://futureforum.com/research/future-forum-pulse
-summer-snapshot/.

177 *As a result, 80 percent:* Morgan Smith, "80% of Bosses Say They Regret Earlier
Return-to-Office Plans: 'A Lot of Executives Have Egg on Their Faces,'" CNBC,
August 14, 2023, https://www.cnbc.com/2023/08/11/80percent-of-bosses-say
-they-regret-earlier-return-to-office-plans.html.

SPECIAL SEGMENT: EXPLORING TOTAL FERTILITY RATE: IMPLICATIONS FOR LEADERSHIP

179 *Economists in the National Bureau of Economic Research:* Martha J. Bailey, Janet
Currie, and Hannes Schwandt, "The Covid-19 Baby Bump: The Unexpected
Increase in U.S. Fertility Rates in Response to the Pandemic," working paper 30569,
National Bureau of Economic Research, October 2022, doi: 10.3386/w30569.

181 *As reported in* Vox: Anna North, "You Can't Even Pay People to Have More
Kids," *Vox,* November 27, 2023, https://www.vox.com/23971366/declining
-birth-rate-fertility-babies-children.

181 *As Gearoid Reidy reports on Bloomberg.com:* Gearoid Reidy, "The Fertility
Crisis Started in Japan, But It Won't Stay There," Bloomberg.com, June 21,
2022, https://www.bloomberg.com/opinion/articles/2022-06-21/the-fertility
-crisis-started-in-japan-but-it-won-t-stay-there.

183 *Women generally bear the brunt:* Emily Field et al., "Women in the Workplace
2023," McKinsey & Company, https://www.mckinsey.com/featured-insights
/diversity-and-inclusion/women-in-the-workplace.

183 *A 2023 Pew Research Center:* Richard Fry, Carolina Aragão, Kiley Hurst, and Kim
Parker, "In a Growing Share of U.S. Marriages, Husbands and Wives Earn About
the Same," Pew Research Center's Social & Demographic Trends Project (blog),
April 13, 2023, https://www.pewresearch.org/social-trends/2023/04/13/in-a
-growing-share-of-u-s-marriages-husbands-and-wives-earn-about-the-same/.

184 *Professor Sanyin Siang:* Sanyin Siang, "The Invisible Roles," Duke Corporate Education, June 1, 2023, https://www.dukece.com/insights/the-invisible-roles/.

CHAPTER 10: FLEXIBILITY: FORTIFY YOUR CULTURE OF GROWTH

192 *Mercer's global survey:* "Health on Demand Survey Report," Mercer, https://
www.mercer.com/en-us/insights/total-rewards/employee-benefits-strategy
/employee-health-survey-health-on-demand/.

192 *A third of pet owners:* "Trouble Keeping or Hiring Employees? Offering Pet

Benefits Could Help!" Nationwide, February 1, 2022, https://news.nationwide
.com/offering-pet-benefits-could-help-keep-employees/.

193 *And this is despite the fact:* Douglas Belkin, "A Generation of American Men
Give Up on College: 'I Just Feel Lost,'" *Wall Street Journal*, September 6,
2021, https://www.wsj.com/articles college-university-fall-higher-education
-men-women-enrollment-admissions-back-to-school-11630948233.

194 *Did you know that:* National Institute on Aging, "Research Explores the Impact
of Menopause on Women's Health and Aging," May 6, 2022, https://www
.nia.nih.gov/news/research-explores-impact-menopause-womens-health
-and-aging.

197 *As researchers at McKinsey write:* Bonnie Dowling, Drew Goldstein, Michael
Park, and Holly Price, "Hybrid Work: Making It Fit with Your Diversity,
Equity, and Inclusion Strategy," McKinsey Quarterly, April 20, 2022, https://
www.mckinsey.com/capabilities/people-and-organizational-performance
/our-insights/hybrid-work-making-it-fit-with-your-diversity-equity-and
-inclusion-strategy.

INDEX

ABOUT THE AUTHOR

Anne Chow is a transformative leader, connector, and innovator who believes that inclusion is foundational to driving strong performance for greater impact. As CEO of AT&T Business, she was the first woman of color CEO in AT&T's over-140-year history. Throughout her trailblazing three-decade career in tech and telecom, she has been an unwavering champion of high-performance teams, strong cultures, equity, and inclusion and is passionate about advancing young women in STEM, advocating for access to education, and investing in next-generation leaders.

She continues her leadership work today in a variety of roles. Chow is the founder and CEO of The Rewired CEO, a business services firm that focuses on powering connection and culture. She serves as lead director on the board of FranklinCovey and is a board member of 3M and CSX. She also teaches at Northwestern University's Kellogg School of Management as a senior fellow and adjunct professor of Executive Education. Among her many accolades, she was named to *Fortune*'s Most Powerful Women in Business List twice and *Forbes* inaugural CEO Next list of up-and-coming leaders set to revolutionize American business. She is a Top Voice on LinkedIn and the bestselling coauthor of *The Leader's Guide to Unconscious Bias: How to Reframe Bias, Cultivate Connection, and Create High-Performance Teams.*

Chow grew up in New Jersey and lives in the Dallas/Fort Worth area. She and her husband, Bob, have two adult daughters and a very spoiled, rescued Australian shepherd.